Financial
Fine Print

Financial Fine Print

Uncovering a Company's True Value

MICHELLE LEDER

WILEY

John Wiley & Sons, Inc.

For general information on our other products and services, or technical support, please contact our Customer Care Department within the United States at 800-762-2974, outside the United States at 317-572-3993, or fax 317-572-4002.

Wiley also publishes its books in a variety of electronic formats. Some content that appears in print may not be available in electronic books.

For more information about Wiley products, visit our web site at *www.wiley.com*.

Library of Congress Cataloging-in-Publication Data

Leder, Michelle.
  Financial fine print : uncovering a company's true value / by Michelle Leder.
    p. cm.
  ISBN 978-0-471-43347-0 (Hardcover) ISBN 978-1-119-09026-7 (Paperback)
  1. Corporations—Valuation. 2. Corporations—Finance. I. Title.
  HG4028.V3L43 2003
  332.63'2042--dc21   2003010886

10 9 8 7 6 5 4 3 2 1

In memory of Al and Hannah Gilden,
my wonderful grandparents, who taught me
that there's much more to life than money

NOTE TO THE READER

Throughout this book, material is provided by financial experts as quoted from interviews conducted by the author. Identification of the source is provided in these instances by an immediate reference to the person interviewed.

CONTENTS

Contents

FOREWORD

BASED ON MY over 40 years of investing in the stock market
and my career on Wall Street engaged in the full-time
analysis of financial statements, it is my opinion that *Financial Fine
Print: Uncovering a Company's True Value* is one of the most inform-
ative books ever written for investors. *Financial Fine Print* enables
investors to become their own forensic accountants, helping them
to navigate the labyrinth associated with the increasingly complex
financial reports of U.S. corporations.

What comes out in the footnotes of a company's financial
reports speaks volumes about a company's real financial health.
Details about many of the big corporate scandals that have domi-
nated headlines in recent years and which have caused many
investors to lose faith in the stock market were actually discussed,
albeit in a limited fashion, in the footnotes of the financial reports
filed with the Securities and Exchange Commission. Whether it was
Adelphia Communications, HealthSouth, and WorldCom disclosing large loans and loan guarantees to insiders, unusual "related
party transactions" at Enron, or aggressive accounting practices at
Tyco International, investors who read the footnotes probably
would have gleaned enough information to keep away from these
troubled stocks or at least to sell them before the bottom fell out.

During the 1990s, it was hard not to get swept up in the euphoria over the stock market, particularly here, in the San Francisco Bay area, where I saw many young companies spring to life. Even for someone who has built his career observing (and often popping) stock market bubbles, it often seemed hard to believe that the good times would ever end. Why would investors pay any attention to the "quality of earnings"—something I spent 30 years writing about—when it didn't even seem to matter whether a company was even reporting earnings? Unfortunately, too many people have learned the hard way—by watching their investments disappear—that the devil often lurks in the details.

While I've long been known for my skeptical views, even I never would have imagined that a company as large as Enron—at the time it was the seventh largest in the country—could have been engaged in such financial chicanery. I often wonder what one of my early mentors, Leonard Spacek, the former chairman of Arthur Andersen & Co., would have made of Enron's confusing footnote on its "related party transactions"—a footnote that had to have been approved by Andersen accountants. I wish that Mr. Spacek, who was an avid critic of creative accounting, had been able to hear what must have been an interesting behind-the-scenes battle between Enron's management and the Andersen auditors over what to include in that footnote. Given his long-held views that accountants "have a professional responsibility to the public," I'm sure that things would have turned out differently for both Enron and Andersen if he had had anything to do with it.

When Enron's former Chief Executive, Jeffrey Skilling, testified before Congress that he was "not an accountant" and could not possibly be expected to understand the financial statements for a company that he had run, he may have deceived investors yet again.

Even if that does prove to be a successful defense for Mr. Skilling, investors need to know that having a Harvard MBA or some other advanced degree is not a prerequisite to understanding the stocks that they own.

"The CEO, if he or she wants to obfuscate, they can do that; and if they want to make it clear, they can do that," says investing guru Warren Buffett. "If they want to provide you with fluff, they can do that. And if they want to provide you with substance, they can do that too."*

Investors who read *Financial Fine Print* will be amply rewarded with the ability to see through the fluff and develop their own red flags after delving through the footnotes. While learning these new skills and putting them to use may take some extra time, I believe it will be time well spent. In their best-selling book *The Millionaire Next Door*, Dr. Thomas J. Stanley and Dr. William D. Danko note that people who spend just a little more time analyzing their investments achieve much better results than their neighbors who do not. *Financial Fine Print* is an invaluable tool that will help investors analyze their own portfolio and teach you how to ask critical questions about the next "must-have" stock.

Happy investing!

Thornton "Ted" Oglove
Author
Quality of Earnings
(Free Press, 1987)
San Francisco
April 2003

---

* U.S. Securities Exchange Commission, "Roundtable Discussion on Financial Disclosure and Auditor Oversight," March 4, 2002 (transcript).

ACKNOWLEDGMENTS

$\mathbf{T}$HERE WERE MANY people who believed in the need for this book from the start, who believed that in order for individual investors to regain their trust, investors needed to gain a better understanding of the stocks in their own portfolios. Chief among those is Thornton "Ted" Oglove, whom I cold-called one day in the fall of 2002 and who has since turned into a trusted friend. Ted's knowledge and experience, and his willingness to share both with me, have been instrumental in writing this book. Dozens of money managers and stock analysts, many of whom preferred to speak on background, also shared their strategies for reading Securities and Exchange Commission filings. Pat McConnell at Bear Stearns and Robert Olstein of Olstein & Associates were particularly helpful and repeatedly made themselves available to answer my many questions. In my research, I was assisted by two diligent research assistants, Aixin "Linda" Liang and Gene Ostrovsky, who plowed through countless 10-Ks and 10-Qs, despite heavy school workloads of their own. This research was enhanced by the access provided to us by *10kwizard.com*. Several people—friends, family, and fellow journalists—provided critical feedback on early chapters: John Bicknell, Emily DeNitto, Carole Flegel, Lisa Lee Freeman, Lauren Gellman, Louis Gilden, Caitlin Mollison, and Mark Walsh. I'd also like to thank Roy Kaufman, a longtime friend who introduced me to my editor, Tim Burgard, who was excited about this book from the start. Tim was a calming influence and, together with my agent, Susan Barry, helped me to navigate my first book. Production editor Sujin Hong went above and beyond the call of duty answering my many questions and making helpful suggestions to improve the book's look. My husband, Scott Cooper, who didn't even have a checking account when we first met, was amazingly supportive and encouraging throughout, as was my stepfather, Barry Montauk. Finally, this book would have been impossible without my mother, Ruth Gilden, who has always been there for me. In addition to being on call to provide research assistance, editing, and even on-site catering, she was and continues to be a constant source of strength and support.

INTRODUCTION

IFIRST LEARNED HOW important footnotes were to uncovering a company's true financial condition back in 1991, when I was a business reporter for *The Bradenton Herald*, a daily newspaper on Florida's west coast. It was at the height of the savings and loan crisis and rumors had been circulating that a small bank based in Bradenton, Key Florida Bank, now long out of business, was cooking its books. Making the story even more interesting was that many of Key's executives, including the chief executive, had worked for another nearby bank, Palmetto Savings and Loan, that federal banking regulators had charged with cooking its books. A year earlier, Palmetto's chief executive had been convicted of bank fraud and sentenced to three years in prison.

Even though Key was a public company, it was not listed on any of the national stock markets and, as a result, did not have to file 10-Ks and 10-Qs with the Securities and Exchange Commission (SEC). But the savings bank did put out an annual report that one

1

employee was nice enough to give me, since this was before the Internet and the report was available only to shareholders. Inside the report was a glowing letter from the bank's president and several charts that showed how profits at the bank were growing.

But it wasn't until I reached the footnotes, where in very small print at the end of the report, the bank disclosed that it had been forced to enter into an operating agreement with the Office of Thrift Supervision (OTS), a federal regulatory agency that was responsible for cleaning up the savings and loan crisis. The footnote went on to say that OTS inspectors believed that Key was violating the agreement and would be subject to further regulatory actions, including possibly closing the bank down. Still, even in those footnotes, Key executives downplayed the situation to shareholders:

> The savings bank has been informed by the OTS, that in the opinion of the OTS, the savings bank has failed to comply with the agreement, which failure of compliance could result in further regulatory action. Management believes the savings bank is in compliance, in all material respects, with the agreement.

Given how regulators were closing savings banks left and right at the time, that kind of disclosure should have sent Key shareholders running for the exits. When regulators moved to shut a bank down, deposits were guaranteed up to $100,000, but shareholders lost everything. Yet most of the shareholders I spoke to at the time, including several of Key's board members, seemed unaware of the bank's shaky financial condition. Few had taken the time to read the footnotes, so they weren't aware that the OTS was cracking down on the bank. One member of Key's board of directors even told me that it wasn't his job to read and understand the bank's financial statements. He was simply on the board to try to spread the word about the bank to colleagues in the area and, it was hoped, bring new business to the bank.

But it was those footnotes that prompted me to take a closer look at the company's numbers. What I found was that the bank was eking out a profit each year by selling assets, rather than making money from its loans and deposits. The financials also revealed that Key's bad loans had been rising sharply, but that the bank's reserves for those bad loans were being whittled down.

Several months later, OTS regulators forced the bank into a more stringent operating agreement and ordered Key's board to fire the chief executive and several other top managers. But for me, it was an early lesson in how some companies use the footnotes as a way to disclose potentially damaging information.

Unfortunately, I forgot about the lessons that I learned from Key when I began investing. Though I had been writing about the stock market for close to a decade as a business journalist and owned several mutual funds, I had never bought an individual stock. But, in the mid-1990s, prompted by the ease of being able to trade online, I bought my first stock, and quickly followed it up with several more. Like many of the millions of other people who were entering the market for the first time, I was so swept up in the excitement of watching the few stocks that I owned rise that I forgot to pay attention to some of the warning signs.

I relied on optimistic projections from stock analysts who appeared on television, even though I knew that their loyalties often were tied to juicy investment banking deals. And instead of reading the detailed filings with their audited financial information, I skimmed the quarterly press releases, which were chock-full of words like pro forma earnings and EBITDA,* vague terms that should have prompted me to take a closer look at the company's audited financials.

Sometimes the difference between the two numbers was literally night and day. For example, Qwest Communications, which I bought in late 1999, routinely touted its quarterly pro forma earnings, as it did in early 2001, when it reported $995 million in what it called net income for 2000, a 53.6 percent increase over 1999. I can still remember thinking how impressive that sounded and practically gloated when the stock started climbing. But had I taken the time to read the 10-K that came out about two months later, I would have seen that Qwest had really lost $81 million for the year, under the rules of generally accepted accounting principles (GAAP), compared with the $1.34 billion in net income it reported in 1999. Such a huge difference between the two figures would have certainly prompted me—and I'm guessing many other investors—to dump the stock long before it fell as sharply as it did.

The Qwest discovery made me begin to wonder whether being more diligent and taking more time before pressing the buy button on my computer screen would have prevented at least some of my losses. What I found in several filings, were questionable related party transactions with company insiders, options and pensions being used to prop up earnings, and other red flags that probably would have prompted me to dump the stock, if only I had taken the time to at least skim the filings.

---

* Earnings before interest, taxes, depreciation, and amortization, or as Lynn Turner, former chief accountant at the SEC, calls them, everything but the bad stuff.

4

That's what this book is all about. It's designed to help other investors navigate what many have been led to believe are complex filings by explaining the hidden meaning in the fine print. No, you won't be able to catch every potential problem. But you can learn to be a more informed investor and learn how to avoid investing in companies that push the accounting envelope.

Even if it takes you a while to pick up these new language skills, chances are you'll be able to spot some potential red flags that can be damaging to your financial health. Because the simple fact is that if you want to own individual stocks, you need to do your homework.

CHAPTER 1

Don't Get Fooled Again

REMEMBER WHEN PICKING winning stocks seemed virtually idiot-proof? You'd catch an analyst on TV, glimpse a headline in some newspaper or magazine, or listen in awe as one of your neighbors boasted about how they had managed to double their money in less than a year. Doubled in less than a year! And then you'd click a button or two on your computer and buy 100 shares, or maybe even more, if you were feeling bullish that day. After all, time was a-wasting and there was money to be made.

If you were feeling particularly ambitious, maybe you spent a few extra minutes and skimmed the company's most recent earnings release, just to make sure things were as rosy as you thought they were. Or maybe you checked out an online message board to see what other investors had to say about the company. Still, you didn't want to waste too much time on research, or you'd never be able to afford your own tropical island, just like that tow truck driver had done in that commercial for one of the big online brokerage firms. Wasn't ignorance bliss?

Now, of course, things look and feel very different. After a spate of multibillion-dollar accounting scandals that have tarnished many on Wall Street (not to mention much of the accounting profession) and a steady drumbeat of companies restating billions of dollars in earnings, it's hard for individual investors to know whom or what to believe anymore. Meanwhile, the list of people whom many of us feel we can no longer trust—accountants, analysts, corporate executives, financial commentators, professional money managers, regulators, and stockbrokers—seems to keep growing every day.

We've learned the hard way—by looking at our monthly brokerage account statements—that the myriad people we were counting on to advise and protect us haven't exactly been doing such a great job.

So whom can this country's 85 million individual investors count on? It would have to be someone who can't be influenced by a hodge-podge of lobbying groups or be tempted by million-dollar bonuses or even hefty stock options—all of which are designed to maintain the status quo.

The answer is amazingly simple: *ourselves.* For individual investors who are willing to put some time and a bit more effort into doing our own research, there's plenty of information available to help us make our own informed decisions and, perhaps more important, avoid much of the hype that surrounds the business of investing.

Granted, we should have been doing this from the beginning. But it was hard not to get swept up in the euphoria of the moment. Certainly, lots of other people did. And since so many of us were new to investing—35 million investors entered the market for the first time during the late 1990s boom—many of us didn't understand the way things really worked. We didn't stop to ask what type of earnings the companies that we invested in were reporting— operating, pro forma, normalized, or some variation on the theme—just so long as they were going up. Sometimes it didn't even matter if the company had any earnings at all. We didn't realize that some of the big-name stock analysts who were talking up stocks in public were secretly bashing them in private. Some of us even honestly thought that with the advent of Internet trading, we could quit our real jobs and count our money all day long.

We won't get fooled again.

One of the few benefits from the wave of accounting scandals that have swept the country is that many companies are now going to great lengths to demonstrate that they're not another Enron or WorldCom. They're providing much more detailed financial information than they ever did before. The bad news is that much of that information is being buried in the fine print in the annual (10-K) and quarterly (10-Q) reports that companies file with the Securities and Exchange Commission (SEC).

Unlike the glossy annual reports with smiling executives and rising bar graphs that individual investors tend to be more familiar with, little of the material in these documents makes for easy reading, at least at first.* There are no colorful charts or pictures—just lots of small black type that seems written in some strange variation of English called accounting-speak. In addition, because the 10-Ks and 10-Qs come out weeks or even months after a company first reports its earnings, many investors mistakenly believe these reports are old news.

---

* A study in August 2002 by Dr. Deanna Oxender Burgess, an accounting professor at Florida Gulf Coast University, found that at least 10 percent of the graphics that appeared in annual reports did not accurately represent the actual numbers.

Yet because the 10-Ks and 10-Qs are subject to SEC scrutiny, they present a much more complete picture of the company than a quarterly or annual earnings press release does and should be considered a must-read for people who want to pick their own stocks. Although professional money managers and analysts have been reading these SEC filings for decades, most individual investors are not very familiar with them. In an effort to make these documents more accessible to their shareholders, some companies have begun posting them on their corporate web sites and sometimes even mailing 10-Ks directly to shareholders in place of the more elaborate annual reports.

There are a few key sections that investors should pay attention to in the 10-Ks, including the Management's Discussion and Analysis (MD&A) and the risk factors. But professional money managers tend to skip over much of this and focus the bulk of their time on the really fine print—the footnotes. In a nutshell, the footnotes provide context for the numbers that appear in the company's key financial tables: the income statement, the balance sheet, and the statement of cash flows. Because they tell the story behind the story, they are critical to understanding a company's true financial health.

"Too many companies would prefer that you not read the footnotes," notes former SEC Chairman Arthur Levitt. "That should be incentive enough to delve into them."[1]

While accounting rules require companies to provide details about how they arrive at many of the key numbers that investors tend to focus on—such as income and revenues—nothing requires companies to make this information easy to find. As a result, most of these details are buried in the footnotes. Companies point this out to investors at the bottom of their financial statements, where a one-line note typically states: "The accompanying notes are an integral part to the consolidated financial statements."

Some companies have begun to provide helpful hints in their financial statements directing investors to a specific footnote in order to get a better understanding of a particular number. Exhibit 1.1 is an example from General Motors' balance sheet in its 2002 10-K.

Enron, for example, disclosed several details on its off-balance sheet transactions—complicated deals that pumped up its earnings and kept debt off the company's balance sheet—in the footnotes to its 1999 and 2000 10-Ks. It was those deals that led to the company's unraveling. Even though the disclosures weren't particularly clear, some savvy investors picked up on them early on and were able to avoid getting burned, as most of Enron's shareholders and employees did. (For more on this, see Chapter 2.)

EXHIBIT 1.1

Helpful Hints from
General Motors 2002 10-K

Years Ended December 31,	2002	2001	2000
(dollars in millions)			
GENERAL MOTORS CORPORATION AND SUBSIDIARIES			
Total net sales and revenues (Notes 1, 2 and 23)	$186,763	$177,260	$184,632
Cost of sales and other expenses (Notes 2 and 3)	153,344	144,093	145,664
Selling, general, and administrative expenses	23,624	23,302	22,252
Interest expense (Note 13)	7,715	8,347	9,552

The bankrupt energy trading company was hardly the first company in the history of the markets to disclose questionable accounting practices in its footnotes. For years, decades even, companies have used the footnotes to bury all sorts of unusual transactions, hoping that as few people as possible would notice. Professional investors, analysts, accountants, and regulators were all aware of how things worked. But sometime during the 1990s, fueled by a raging bull market, the people who normally read those footnotes—who were being paid to read them—either stopped or didn't bother to ask questions about what they were reading.

"Everyone went into a period of suspended disbelief. It was like going to the movies. Nobody was paying attention," says Lynn Turner, the former chief accountant at the SEC who now teaches at Colorado State University's Center for Quality Financial Reporting. "Now it's like walking out of the movie theater and into reality again. There's a real getting back to basics."

In the wake of the massive accounting scandals, companies are putting much more detailed information into their footnotes and in their disclosures in their annual proxy statements. Although some of that is probably designed to protect companies from future investor lawsuits, this greater level of disclosure also benefits investors at all levels of sophistication—from novice to expert. Still, all of this additional information doesn't mean very much unless we take the time to read it.

For example, General Electric Corp., which has long been considered by many professional investors to have some of the most confusing financial statements, provided its investors with 57 percent more pages of financial information in its 2002 10-K than it did in its 2000 filing, the year before Enron imploded. During that time, the number of pages devoted to footnotes increased by over 20 percent.

For all of the companies in the Dow 30, the average number of pages devoted to footnotes in their 10-Ks grew 23 percent between 2001 and 2002 and was up 77 percent from five years earlier. (See Exhibit 1.2.) Companies also are disclosing much more information in the footnotes to their 10-Qs, some of which are now almost as long as 10-Ks used to be. Dick Weiss, who co-manages the $2.5 billion Strong Opportunity Fund, says that 10-Qs never used to provide him with much useful information, but he's noticed a significant change in recent years.

This growth trend seems likely to continue. Indeed, a survey by *CFO* magazine in August 2002 found that 59 percent of the senior financial executives surveyed already had begun to disclose more information in their financial statements over the past three months; 72 percent of that increased disclosure took place in the footnotes.[2] Asked whether they planned to disclose more information over the next 12 months, 57 percent of executives answered yes, and 70 percent indicated that the additional disclosure would take place in the footnotes.

That sharp increase has prompted many professional investors to devote dozens of hours to reading and analyzing these additional pages of disclosure before making an investment decision.

"I want those Ks and Qs read from the back," says J. Thomas Madden, vice chairman for investment management at Federated Investors, which manages about $25 billion. "I want you to read the footnotes first. If you go to one less analyst conference sponsored by some [Wall] Street firm in order to sit in your office reading footnotes and asking tough questions about what those footnotes do and don't say, you're going to be much more likely to catch the next problem."[3]

Even for those relatively new to investing, reading the footnotes isn't as daunting as it might seem at first blush. Yes, the type

Trends in the Number of Pages for Footnotes in 10-Ks for Dow 30 Companies

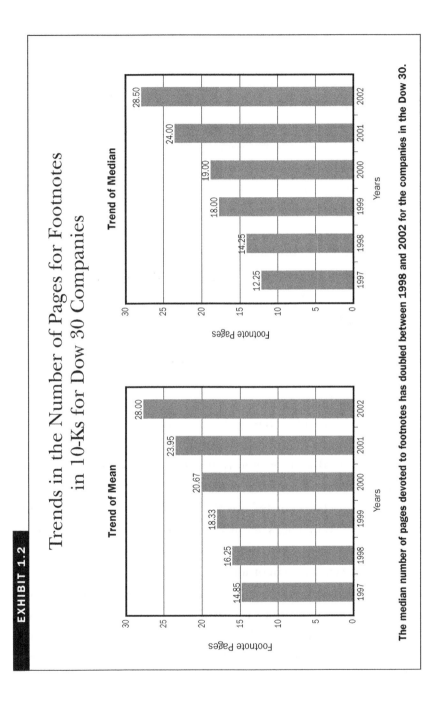

Trend of Mean

Trend of Median

The median number of pages devoted to footnotes has doubled between 1998 and 2002 for the companies in the Dow 30.

14

is small and the words may seem unfamiliar. But don't let that stop you. First, there's no need to read the footnotes word for word. As you'll see throughout this book, there are ways to take shortcuts and still get a sense on whether a company is being overly aggressive when it comes to the numbers it is reporting. Simply looking at the interest rate that a company uses to calculate its pension assets—something that takes a few seconds at best once you know where to look—can tell you whether a company is likely to be aggressive in other areas too. (For a more complete discussion of pensions, see Chapter 7.)

If you're a typical investor, you probably assume that the generally accepted accounting principles, or GAAP, which companies follow when reporting their results, are ironclad rules that leave little room for interpretation. But in reality, these "rules" leave lots of wiggle room for companies looking to take a more aggressive approach when it comes to their accounting practices. In a nutshell, earnings as defined by GAAP require a company's management to make all sorts of assumptions that can have a sizable impact on revenues and expenses, producing very different numbers if those assumptions are wrong. As a result, two identical companies (assuming there were such a thing) could report vastly different results, simply by making different assumptions as allowed under GAAP, notes Thornton "Ted" Oglove. Oglove's groundbreaking 1987 book, *Quality of Earnings*, described the many ways that public companies manipulate accounting rules to present their financial results in the best possible light.

"Companies are legally manipulating their earnings and nobody is ever going to be able to stop them from doing it," says Oglove. "Management whitewashes everything."

For example, Tyco International, the conglomerate whose chief executive officer and chief financial officer were charged by federal prosecutors with orchestrating a $600 million fraud, announced in December 2002 that it had done nothing more than engage in "a pattern of using aggressive accounting."[4] Investors who had taken the time to read Tyco's footnotes in earlier SEC filings might have been able to pick up on unusual accounting patterns related to the company's many acquisitions. In 1998, for example, Tyco disclosed that it had spent $4.2 billion to acquire different companies and then also disclosed that it had written off $4.1 billion in goodwill and other merger-related expenses.[5] In later years, these numbers only grew larger.

Getting a handle on the nuances of GAAP and its thousands of pages of rules is simply too much for most investors, even for many pros. What individual investors can learn, however, are the techniques that companies use to present their earnings and other so-called headline numbers—the numbers that most often appear in news reports—in the best possible light.

Weiss, of the Strong Opportunity Fund, says he's seen companies report a 25 percent increase in operating earnings to investors, only to do some quick calculations after the 10-K or 10-Q came out and realize that the company's results were actually negative. "You can have a company report good results, but then you start doing adjustments and you realize that things aren't as they seem," says Weiss.

Some people want you to believe that reading 10-Ks and 10-Qs is next to impossible, that you need to have a background in finance, be a certified public accountant, and have a solid understanding of the many accounting rules put out by the Financial Accounting Standards Board (FASB). None of that would hurt, of course, but chances are that anyone who's telling you that reading the Ks and Qs is too difficult has a vested interest in keeping you uninformed. If that's the case, you had better hope that you're paying that person enough money to read these filings for you.

Even as Ks and Qs continue to grow in size and complexity, it shouldn't take more than an hour to skim a K once you understand what you're supposed to be looking for. A typical Q should take about 15 minutes. To figure out whether this is worth your time, just think about how much an hour of your time is normally worth. Chances are that an hour spent reading a K and spotting potential problems will more than pay for itself.

These reports are accessible online from many different web sites, including *www.10kwizard.com*, a good site because it enables investors to skip to the footnotes quickly, as well as the SEC's own site *www.sec.gov*. In addition, many companies post the reports on their own corporate web sites or provide links to other sites that enable investors to access the filings.

While there are many different techniques for reading a 10-K, depending on an individual's investment style, many professional investors start reading these filings from the back to the front, reading the footnotes even before they read the financials. By skimming the footnotes for red flags, such as aggressive accounting policies, as was the case with Tyco, many pros are able to make a quick decision on whether it pays to invest additional time on research.

"We're much more interested in what the numbers mean, rather than what the numbers are," says Marty Whitman, co-chief investment officer of the Third Avenue Value Fund and a long-time critic of aggressive accounting. "It's sort of a translation thing. The audited financial statements do not and cannot be expected to tell us the truth. We use them as tools to discover our own version of the truth."

Jim Chanos, a New York–based hedge fund manager who was one of the first professional investors to bet big money that Enron was a house of cards, uncovered many of the company's problems by reading the footnotes in Enron's SEC filings.

"Earnings as defined in the U.S. are subject to lots of assumptions that management can make. In order to figure out those assumptions, you have to go beyond the earnings to the financial statements and then beyond that to the footnotes to understand what assumptions management is making," says Chanos. "Just looking at the balance sheet, cash flow, and profit and loss statement is not enough anymore. Too many companies are putting too much information into their footnotes."

CHAPTER 2

Reading the
Fine Print
Like a Pro

W HEN ENRON BEGAN to implode in the fall of 2001, many investment professionals—analysts, brokers, financial planners, and money managers—said they were shocked—shocked!—to learn the news. After all, the company had been consistently reporting higher revenues and earnings, and its stock had developed a cultlike status. Even when the company filed for bankruptcy on December 2, 2001—by that time Enron had already disclosed significant accounting problems—many analysts still seemed surprised, judging by the number who continued to rate the stock as a buy. In addition, more than 400 mutual funds owned Enron shares just prior to the company filing for bankruptcy.[1]

"Everyone was asleep at the switch," says Ted Oglove. "Even after [Chief Executive Officer Jeff] Skilling left, nobody bothered to read the footnotes."

Well, maybe not everyone. One of the few people who had anticipated problems at Enron a full year before they became apparent was Jim Chanos, who manages over $1 billion in assets for his company, Kynikos Associates. Though he initially thought Enron was simply engaged in aggressive accounting, rather than a sophisticated accounting fraud, Chanos says he knew that something wasn't quite right after carefully reading Enron's Securities and Exchange Commission (SEC) filings. Focusing in on the footnotes in Enron's 10-Ks and 10-Qs, Chanos and his group of six analysts spent time reading and rereading the documents and found some of the disclosures puzzling, even for a group of grizzled pros used to tweezing out information from these seemingly dull reports.

The focus of Kynikos, which in Greek means "cynic," is to find overvalued companies and then short those stocks. Shorting a stock basically means betting that the stock price will go down instead of up. The many critics of this investing technique—and there are many—say that short sellers exploit the negatives in order to make money. Some critics have even gone as far as to call short-sellers unpatriotic. Among those critics was former Enron CEO Skilling, who, during a conference call with analysts to discuss first-quarter earnings in April 2001, called one short seller an a__hole after being questioned as to why Enron didn't have a cash-flow statement or balance sheet available.[2]

RED FLAG

Be careful when a company starts bashing short sellers. It could be a sign of more serious problems ahead.

Even if you're not a big fan of short selling as an investment strategy, this type of research-intensive approach to picking stocks provides many valuable lessons for individual investors who are

 **IN FOCUS**

It's an understatement to say that most executives at publicly traded companies—whose job, among other things, is to boost the stock price—are not enamored with short sellers, who profit when the stock price falls. But when management declares war against the shorts, ordinary investors should strongly consider selling their shares. A 2002 study by University of Chicago business school professor Owen A. Lamont looked at 270 companies over 25 years and found that those companies that had waged public wars against short sellers saw their stocks decline more than 2 percent *a month* over the next 12 months.[*] Companies that claimed that short sellers were involved in a conspiracy—a fairly common complaint—lost nearly 4 percent a month, something most individual investors probably would rather avoid. So when Enron's CEO used an off-color remark to criticize short seller Richard Grubman of Highfields Capital Management during an analysts' conference call in April 2001, other investors would have been wise to consider that a strong sell signal. On April 17, the day of that call, Enron shares closed at $60. Nearly four months later, when Skilling unexpectedly resigned, the stock had declined by nearly 30 percent. Not quite four months after that, Enron filed for bankruptcy, making its shares essentially worthless.

[*] Owen A. Lamont, "Go Down Fighting: Short Sellers vs. Firms," University of Chicago, January 2003. Working Paper.

basically bullish but would like to avoid future disasters. Instead of wasting time listening to company executives spin their numbers during conference calls or reading analysts' reports, many short sellers focus on the company's SEC filings, primarily the footnotes in the 10-Ks and 10-Qs, which take time to read and analyze. By mining these documents for discrepancies and looking for unusually worded disclosures, short sellers say it's often possible to pick up on problems long before others do.

That's not to say that this approach always works. Many times it's simply too difficult to predict how serious a particular problem is or how other investors will react. Sometimes it's even difficult to find the problem in the first place. Still, before a company goes into a free fall, it usually leaves some telltale clues that observant investors often are able to pick up on. That's particularly true now with companies disclosing more than ever before. Understanding what professionals look for when they dive into the footnotes can help individual investors make more educated decisions.

Just by looking at Chanos's copy of Enron's 1999 10-K filing, which he picked up for the first time in the fall of 2000, you can tell that this wasn't a quick read.* Dozens of yellow Post-it notes stick out from the pages, highlighting sections that Chanos and his team of analysts paid extra attention to. Throughout the filing, numbers on the income statement and in the footnotes are circled in pencil and some, including Enron's now-famous Footnote 16, which provided sketchy details on the off-balance sheet deals that eventually brought the company down, are underlined and punctuated by question marks and exclamation points. (See Exhibit 2.1.)

"If one of us doesn't understand a footnote, that's a red flag," says Chanos. "We understand a lot of them, but every now and then, there's one that throws us for a loop."

---

* The idea, in this age of real-time numbers and analysis, that something like a 10-K could still be useful more than six months after its release is an important one for individual investors to think about. Many individual investors, particularly those who first became interested in the market during the Internet boom, tend to approach investing like the 100-yard dash, where speed is everything. But sometimes the tortoise really can beat the hare, simply by being a little bit smarter.

EXHIBIT 2.1

Enron Footnote 16 from 1999 10-K

In June 1999, Enron entered into a series of transactions involving a third party and LJM Cayman L.P. (LJM). LJM is a private investment company which engages in acquiring or investing in primarily energy-related investments. A Senior officer of Enron is the managing member of LJM's general partner. The effect of the transactions was (i) Enron and the third party amended certain forward contracts to purchase shares of Enron common stock, resulting in Enron having forward contracts to purchase Enron stock at the market price of that day, (ii) LJM received 6.8 million shares of Enron common stock subject to certain restrictions and, (iii) Enron received a note receivable and certain financial instruments hedging an investment held by Enron. Enron recorded the assets received and equity issued at estimated fair value. In connection with the transactions, LJM agreed that the Enron officer would have no pecuniary interest in such Enron common shares and would be restricted from voting on matters related to such shares. LJM repaid the note receivable in December 1999. LJM2 Co-Investment L.P. (LJM2) was formed in December 1999 as a private investment company which engages in acquiring or investing in primarily energy-related or communications-related businesses. In the fourth quarter of 1999, LJM2, which has the same general partner as LJM, acquired, directly or indirectly, approximately $360 million of merchant assets and investments from Enron, on which Enron recognized pre-tax gains of approximately $16 million. In December 1999, LJM2 entered into an agreement to acquire Enron's interests in an unconsolidated equity affiliate for approximately $34 million. Additionally, LJM acquired assets from Enron for $11 million. At December 31, 1999, JEDI held approximately

(continues)

EXHIBIT 2.1 *(CONTINUED)*

12 million shares of Enron Corp. common stock. The value of the Enron Corp. common stock has been hedged. In addition, an officer of Enron has invested in the limited partner of JEDI and from time to time acts as agent on behalf of the limited partner's management. In 1999, Whitewing acquired approximately $192 million of merchant assets from Enron. Enron recognized no gains or losses in connection with these transactions. Management believes that the terms of the transactions with related parties are representative of terms that would be negotiated with unrelated third parties.

After reading both the 1998 10-K and the proxy statement, which made no reference to any of the off-balance sheet transactions, it became clear to Chanos that this disclosure was an important new development at Enron that was certainly worth investigating further. Even though the footnote provided only a rough outline of the complicated web of transactions that moved debt off Enron's balance sheet, it was unusual enough to prompt Chanos to start shorting the stock in the fall of 2000. While off-balance sheet transactions were not all that uncommon, at the time few companies provided many details about them, even in their footnotes. The fact that Enron seemed to be going out of its way to disclose this string of interrelated companies and specifically mentioned that one of its senior officers was a principal of several, was another critical clue for Chanos.

 RED FLAG

If after reading a section in a 10-K or 10-Q several times you still don't understand it, chances are the company is trying to confuse you.

In its quarterly SEC filings for March, June, and September 2000, as well as its 2000 10-K and proxy, which came out in the spring of 2001, Enron provided some additional details on these unusual business dealings. Enron's Related Party Transactions footnote in its 2000 10-K was more than twice as long as the one that had appeared a year earlier. The company provided still more details on these interconnected transactions in its 2000 proxy, something it had not done before. Over the course of two years, this particular footnote in the 10-K had grown from nothing to more than one and a half pages of fine print, a clear sign that this was something worth paying attention to.

"Any time management seems like it is going out of its way to tell you something, that's a red flag," says Chanos. "I'm sure that Enron's management probably didn't want to write that related party trans-action footnote, but they were probably forced to by the lawyers."

Robert Olstein, of the Olstein Financial Alert Fund, which focuses on investing in beaten-up companies that have strong bal-ance sheets, says he looked at Enron carefully as the stock was falling in mid-2001 but wound up passing after reading Footnote 16. "There was so much in their special purpose entities [SPEs] that I didn't understand," Olstein says. Considering that Olstein has spent over 30 years picking apart financial statements and reading footnotes, including 10 years working with Ted Oglove on the *Quality of Earnings Report*, it says a lot that he wasn't able to understand the footnote completely. So he did the only smart thing he could and kept away.

Now, of course, investors know that the problems hinted at in Enron's footnotes were much more serious than anyone could even imagine.

While Enron's related party transactions footnote was by far the biggest warning sign, pros say that other things also stood out in Enron's filings. For example, in Note 12 on pension obligations, Enron disclosed that it was using a 10.5 percent rate of return for its pension assets.[*] Accounting rules say that it's perfectly legal for companies to make their own assumptions here. But for a pension fund with hundreds of millions of dollars in it—Enron's stood at $853 million at the end of 1999—even an extra half of 1 percent could add millions to the company's income statement. (For a more complete discussion on pensions, see Chapter 7.)

That's one of the reasons why professional money managers like Chanos and Olstein, who read 10-Ks on an almost daily basis, say that pension footnotes can be a strong (and relatively quick) signal to individual investors as to whether a company is engaging in aggressive accounting. Olstein, for example, says that when he started to read Lucent Technologies' 10-Ks for 1997 and 1998, he noticed what he considered to be a significant amount of the company's revenues coming from employee pensions. As it turns out, that wasn't the only area where Lucent was being overly aggressive. Poking around a bit more, Olstein saw that Lucent was using reserves to pump up earnings and that receivables and inventories

---

[*] Actually, the 10.5 percent rate was disclosed in a footnote to the pension footnote in Enron's 1999 10-K filing.

were growing faster than sales, prompting him to short Lucent stock, an investing strategy he does relatively infrequently.

"The pension assumption tells you something about the management's conservatism, or lack thereof," says Chanos, who also believes that 6 percent is an appropriate rate of return.

Indeed, many other pros say that the interest rate that companies pick here—remember, this is a number that companies can literally pull out of thin air and place on their income statements —often determines how intensely they'll study the rest of the filing. If the company is using a questionable number here, they say, chances are better than even that the aggressive pattern will repeat itself in other parts of the financial statements.

"It's just one of those triggers," says Liz Fender of TIAA-CREF. "It says more about the attitude and how much the company is willing to push things."

Most pros, in fact, have a "favorite" footnote that they tend to turn to first because it provides a reality check as they read other parts of the report and can help them determine how much time to spend researching a company. Olstein likes to start with the company's footnote on income taxes, because it tells him the difference between a company's reported earnings and its tax earnings, which can be a sign of creative accounting. (For more on this, see Chapter 9.) Others, like Chanos, start at the beginning—usually the description of the company's major accounting policies—and plow straight through.

But there are some ways to take shortcuts. The most important footnote to read varies depending on the company. Pros tend to know which one this is right off the bat, but individuals need to take time to learn. In general, though, it pays to think about a critical piece of the business and look closely at whatever additional disclosure the company provides on the topic. At a large retailer like The Home Depot, the footnote on leases is key. At a technology company like Cisco Systems, which hands out lots of options, it's a good idea to read the options footnote. At a pharmaceutical company like Pfizer, investors should focus on the research and development footnote. And at a company like Tyco, which was basically in the business of acquiring other companies, the critical footnotes tend to be the ones that cover mergers and acquisitions and restructuring costs.

"Different companies have different things that are important," notes Marty Whitman, of the Third Avenue Value Fund.

Chanos says that he spent a lot of time reading Tyco's footnote on acquisitions in several 10-Ks. From that note, he was able to determine that Tyco bought $19 billion worth of companies in 2000 but allocated $21 billion to goodwill, a significant sign of aggresive accounting.

"Either every single company that they bought had a negative net worth when Tyco bought them, or Tyco had the company take charges just before the purchase," says Chanos, who wound up shorting the stock (and profiting handsomely) from his careful reading of Tyco's footnotes. "Now we know that Tyco was engineering all sorts of accounting, even though the company denied this vociferously at the time."

One technique that many pros use to find this buried treasure (or buried garbage) is to line up several years of filings at a time and take special note of any changes, such as a new footnote or one that seems much more detailed than in previous years. Some pros also like to line up several companies in the same industry, say three pharmaceutical companies, and compare their 10-Ks because the accounting tends to be similar, making it easier to spot something unusual.

"You want to look at several 10-Ks over the years," says forensic accountant Tim Mulligan, who publishes *The Green Eyeshade Report* newsletter. "Are things getting better or worse?"

Of course, most individual investors won't be able to devote that kind of time to digging through a company's SEC filings, nor do we need to, unless we're talking about a very substantial investment. Often just skimming two years' worth of 10-Ks side by side and looking for anything new can tell you whether it makes sense to devote additional time to researching the company.

What made Note 16 in Enron's 1999 10-K so interesting was that it was the first time a note like that had appeared in the company's SEC filings. Enron didn't put stars around the footnote or call attention to this change in some other way. But people who did a quick comparison of the 1998 and 1999 10-Ks would have seen that this was new information and, at that point, could have made a decision based on their own investment needs as to whether this was worth paying closer attention to.

Many pros also like to look for any changes in accounting policies from year to year. Typically, the first or second footnote is called "significant accounting policies." This footnote is usually long and full of different accounting rules, creating a bit of an alphabet soup that can seem unsavory. But even if you don't understand every rule—and often even many professionals don't—all you're really looking for here are any changes in either content or scope.

For example, in its 1999 10-K on significant accounting policies, America Online (now AOL Time Warner) devoted two paragraphs to its revenue recognition policies. By 2000, that section had grown to six paragraphs, and in 2001, the first year after the firm merged with Time Warner, the space devoted to revenue recognition stretched on for 16 paragraphs. That alone should have prompted any investor who owned shares of AOL to pay closer attention. Making this disclosure even more important was AOL's track record: In 2000, after an SEC review, the company restated its earnings from 1994 to 1996 over questions having to do with the way it had accounted for expenses. Although the company paid the SEC a $3.5 million fine—the largest ever at the time—it denied any wrongdoing.[3] In mid-2002, AOL restated $190 million in additional revenues and disclosed that both the SEC and the Department of Justice were conducting separate reviews of the company.

Granted, wading through pages of accounting rules and policies isn't particularly enjoyable. But Lynn Turner, the former chief accountant at the SEC, says that even though the accounting-speak in the significant accounting policies footnote tends to make many individual investors' eyes glaze over, it is simply too important for most investors to skip. "It's a good place to find out how aggressive the company is being," Turner says.

Many other pros also consider this footnote critical to understanding the rest of the footnotes. Even reading it quickly can help you understand how far the company is willing to push the accounting envelope. To some extent, it's like playing Monopoly with a group of old friends. You all know how to play the game, but each person's interpretation of the rules may be slightly different, so before the game starts, everyone needs to understand and agree on the rules.

"Management has lots of choices, and this footnote basically lets me pick out the guys who are conservative and the guys who are promotional," says Whitman.

Among the items that pros like Whitman tend to pay particular attention to in this footnote are the company's revenue recognition policies and depreciation rates, two items that can have a huge impact on revenues and expenses. Basic economics (not to mention human nature) dictates that a company wants to maximize revenues and minimize expenses to make earnings look as strong as possible.

Although the rules on revenue recognition and depreciation are long and very complicated, there are really only a few ways that companies can try to puff up their numbers here: by counting revenue that doesn't really exist, by counting revenue too early or too late, and by fiddling around with depreciation rates.

"Half of all financial fiascoes are caused by revenue recognition, usually when the company is being too aggressive," says Pat McConnell, chief accounting analyst at Bear Stearns.

While some investors may be able to spot unusual trends on the income statement, doing this can be difficult for most of us. Yet by reading the relevant parts of the Accounting Policies footnote and looking for any changes from a previous quarter or year, savvy investors may be able to pick up on a potential problem before it becomes a more substantial one.

Between 1997 and 2002, the number of companies restating their financial results more than tripled, according to the federal General Accounting Office (GAO), which also found that the

RED FLAG

Be particularly wary of companies that recognize revenue when items are shipped or use percentage of completion, an accounting term often used on long-term projects. Although there can be legitimate reasons for both, these are two well-known areas of abuse.

average stock price for companies restating their earnings declined by 10 percent on the day following the restatement.[4] In addition, the GAO found that the number of large companies restating their results had risen sharply, as had the size and scope of the restatements.[5] While some restatements have been caused by honest mistakes, the sheer volume of restatements has prompted many pros to take a much more cynical view.

In March 2003, for example, pharmaceutical giant Bristol-Myers Squibb said it had overstated its revenues by $2.5 billion and its earnings by $900 million between 1999 and 2001 because of what it described as "errors and inappropriate accounting." Several months earlier, after the company disclosed that the SEC had launched a formal investigation, Bristol-Myers Squibb said that it had improperly used sales incentives to induce wholesalers to buy its product before the end of a particular quarter.[6]

During the early 1990s, Waste Management took an overly aggressive approach toward depreciation rates, hoping that nobody would notice, and, indeed, few investors caught this item buried in the footnotes. But by taking this approach, Waste Management was able to sharply reduce its expenses, making the company's earnings over several years look better—$1.4 billion better, in fact —than they really were. Although former accounting firm Arthur Andersen eventually wound up paying the SEC a $7 million fine in 2001 and agreed not to break any accounting rules in the future, for years the firm had maintained that it was simply using the flexibility built into GAAP rules.*

---

* It was Arthur Andersen's settlement with the SEC over problems at Waste Management that eventually led to the criminal indictment of the entire firm and hastened its closure. Once regulators and prosecutors began to fully understand the depth of the Enron fiasco, and took into account Andersen's recent pledge following Waste Management, just going after a few partners, instead of the entire firm, would have seemed like a weak solution.

To remind investors about all of the choices management has in picking assumptions that impact earnings, some companies have begun to include in their SEC filings extensive lists of the numbers that are dependent on these management assumptions, so buyer beware. Some pros even joke that these warnings resemble the detailed warning labels on cigarette packages today, although they're not posted quite as prominently. Here's an example from a 10-Q filed by Lucent Technologies on February 11, 2003:

> Among other things, estimates and assumptions are used in accounting for long-term contracts, allowances for bad debts and customer financings, inventory obsolescence, restructuring reserves, product warranty, amortization and impairment of intangibles, goodwill, and capitalized software, depreciation and impairment of property, plant and equipment, employee benefits, income taxes, and contingencies. The company believes that adequate disclosures are made to keep the information presented from being misleading.

A number of companies have begun to move this warning label to the beginning of their footnotes. For example, in Qwest Communications' 2000 10-K filing, this reminder was the second item listed under the accounting policies footnotes. In Qwest's 1999 10-K, it was the next to last item. This serves as a reminder that even when they follow GAAP, companies and their accountants still have plenty of choices to make in applying the rules.

Some companies that have been tarnished by accounting scandals in the past are adding pages of additional notes to explain their accounting policies. For example, Cendant Corp., which in 1998 revealed a $500 million accounting fraud, devoted 10 pages to its accounting policies in its 2001 10-K filing, more than twice the number it used in its 2000 filing. Granted, some of that extra text appears to be mind-numbing legalese, but given the company's history, Cendant shareholders should at least be skimming over this extra disclosure.

One other area that many pros have started to pay a lot more attention to lately is one-time or special charges, something that individual investors have been conditioned to ignore because they're considered to be nonrecurring. Though professional money managers have also largely ignored these items in the past, some are paying a lot more attention as the size and number of "special" charges continues to increase. Some companies end up taking "unusual" charges every quarter. Cendant, for one, took "special" charges during every single quarter between 1998 and 2002, according to Reuters. (For more on this, see Chapter 4.) Although companies say they break out these charges to give investors a clearer view of operating earnings, a string of special charges quarter after quarter often makes it hard to compare results from quarter to quarter or year to year.

"There's a lot of room to play there and it impacts future income," says Jeff Middleswart, who writes the newsletter *Behind the Numbers*, which looks at the hidden meanings in financial statements and is popular with many professional money managers, for David Tice & Associates. "Wall Street and analysts tend to ignore restructuring charges."

Of course, all of this research takes time—sometimes more time than most investors think they have. But it pays to invest your time before investing your money. During the roaring bull market of the 1990s, individual investors thought they had to make snap decisions or risk losing out. But few professionals—people responsible for investing billions of dollars each year—make quick investment decisions when it comes to their own money or the money they're investing for others.

"If we're making an investment decision, you better bet that we're going through things line by line," says Whitman. In order to complete the type of intensive research he prefers, it might take him as long as a week to review a typical 10-K.

Indeed, it's not uncommon for professionals to spend several hours when they pick up a 10-K for the first time. Chanos says he spends at least an hour on a first reading and then spends several additional hours on a second or even a third reading, all the time getting feedback from other analysts on his staff. Olstein says he typically spends one and a half hours the first time he reads a 10-K, even though he reads over 100 a year and has been doing this type of research-intensive investing for the past 35 years.

Although they have different investment strategies—Chanos is focused on short opportunities while Olstein and Whitman look for bargains among beaten-down companies—these pros say they largely ignore what management has to say. While they may listen in during company conference calls with analysts, they'd much rather focus their attention—and their time—on the SEC filings.

"It's going to take the average investor a long time, but they should spend it," Olstein says. "Read the financials. The information is there."

CHAPTER 3

You Don't Need to Be a Pro

INDIVIDUAL INVESTORS LOOKING to do their own research may want to borrow a page from Colette Neuville. A 60-something grandmother in France, Neuville was one of the few investors, and perhaps the only individual investor, to question the accounting practices at Vivendi Universal SA in the months before the company began to implode in mid-2002. Vivendi, which grew from a humble French water utility company to a multinational entertainment conglomerate over the course of a few short years, became the subject of major securities and criminal investigations, as well as shareholder lawsuits, on both sides of the Atlantic in 2002.

Neuville, who is one of the leading advocates for individual investors in France, first began reading the fine print in 1990, after a stock brokerage she had invested in filed for bankruptcy. After organizing other investors and successfully fighting to get their money back, Neuville formed Association pour la Defense des Actionnaires Minoritaires (ADAM), a group dedicated to helping France's growing number of individual investors. Since then she's pored over the financial statements for dozens of companies, including some of the biggest corporate names in France. Sometimes, she even teams up with large institutional investors—something that is still pretty rare in the United States—to demonstrate that both types of investors are capable of working together when it comes to a particular issue.

But the fight over Vivendi was the retired economist's biggest battle by far. At its annual shareholders' meeting in April 2002, Neuville raised numerous questions about Vivendi's financial condition, even though she had had only a few hours to review the report. Unlike American investors, who get access to a company's year-end financials weeks and sometimes even months before an annual meeting, Neuville says that French shareholders typically are given the information the day of the meeting. This all but ensures that shareholders won't be able to ask corporate executives tough questions at the meeting based on the information in the report, Neuville says. Quarterly information, she says, is even sketchier—generally a few headline numbers that appear in a business newspaper or are available online.

After the Vivendi annual meeting, Neuville spent two to three weeks reading the company's results, reviewing the 2001 report thoroughly, and going back several years to look at previous results. She says she was surprised by many of the things that she, with the help of a former Vivendi employee, found buried in the fine print, most notably the company's declining cash position and growing mountain of debt. It was this cash crunch that led to Vivendi's near-death experience. But finding these problems required a bit of digging and a fair amount of cynicism because like many companies, Vivendi seemed to put its best foot forward and hide its most serious problems in the footnotes.

"There's two ways to present financial results," Neuville says. "Optimistically and realistically. Vivendi was presenting their results very optimistically in 2001 and 2002. But it was more than that. When the CEO [chief executive officer] said there was no problem with cash, he was not exactly telling the truth."

On July 1, 2002, about a week after several Vivendi directors were warned by investment banking firm Goldman Sachs that the company would be bankrupt by September or October, Vivendi's charismatic CEO, Jean-Marie Messier, resigned.[1] Shortly before he was forced to step down, Messier offered Neuville a seat on Vivendi's board, one indication that her questions about Vivendi's health were finally being taken seriously.

"Sometimes it's difficult to see everything because the information is not easy to find," says Neuville. "But at Vivendi, the information was buried in the details."

When Neuville started out, she says she knew virtually nothing about reading a financial statement. Although she was trained as an economist, she spent two decades raising her five children. It was only after losing a good chunk of her nest egg that she decided to learn more about investing. Although Neuville says that she didn't have well-honed analytical skills or an advanced degree in finance or accounting, she didn't need them. What she did have was a real passion to avoid future financial fiascoes.

As with Vivendi, many of the companies that have been tarred by accounting scandals in recent years—Enron, WorldCom, Adelphia, Tyco, and HealthSouth—all provided numerous clues in their Securities and Exchange Commission (SEC) filings. Of course, individual investors were not the only ones who missed these hints. Mutual fund managers, analysts, and accountants very clearly missed many of them too. Fidelity Investments, for example, had a huge stake in HealthSouth when that company blew up in March 2003. Jim Chanos, of Kynikos, says that one analyst he talked to about Enron in the months before it imploded admitted that it was difficult to understand how the company made money, but he insisted to Chanos that the company was actually understating its profits instead of grossly overstating them.

"Analysts read the Ks, but with an exception of a small minority, they don't care. They're not there to find negatives," Chanos says.

These repeated misses—by people who were theoretically, at least, being paid to find them—are perhaps the best argument for why individuals need to work on honing our own skills. Clearly, in many cases, it would be hard to do much worse.

"The average investor really needs to start reading these things," says Dick Weiss, co-manager of the $2.5 billion Strong Opportunity Fund. "It's not like you need to be a CPA [certified public accountant] to read them."

Several different studies show that very few individual investors approach financial reports the way that Neuville does. Indeed, at least before the accounting scandals of 2001 and 2002, most of us were apt to take financial results at face value, relying on the company's reported earnings in its press releases, which were often substantially different than those provided in the company's SEC filings.

During the 1990s, when companies were routinely touting pro forma results—a term that has no real meaning—and talking about new metrics for measuring a company, few investors raised questions. Several studies even showed that the average investor spent more time researching a new car, a major appliance, or even a place to eat dinner than on researching investments. Those of us who did do some research didn't tend to look much further than newspaper and magazine articles or reports by stock analysts— reports that were rarely, if ever, negative. Footnotes weren't exactly on our radar screens.

"Everyone was making so much money that nobody wanted to rock the boat," says Lynn Turner, the former chief accountant at the SEC. "And anyone who raised questions about the questionable accounting got shot."

One study by Cornell University's Johnson School of Business Professor Robert J. Bloomfield found that many investors tend to assume—wrongly—that because the footnotes appear at the end of the report and are in a smaller typeface, they must be less important.[2]

But because many professional money managers tend to spend a good deal of their time on the footnotes, more so now post-Enron, this dichotomy creates what Bloomfield calls an incomplete information hypothesis, where professional investors have better information simply because they take the time to read the fine print and understand what they're reading. By doing so, they transfer wealth from less-informed investors to those who are more informed. "There's an informational advantage for people who know how to read this," Bloomfield says. "Companies know that if they put something in a footnote, fewer people will see it."

Jack Ciesielski, a frequent accounting critic who writes a newsletter for analysts and institutional investors called the *Analysts Accounting Observer*, says there's no shortage of important information for investors who are willing to put in the time. Unfortunately, however, many of us seem to doubt our own ability to research our investments more fully.

One of the biggest problems many investors face is that it can be hard to figure out what's important in the fine print. Even pros who are experienced at reading the footnotes face this problem. And now that so many companies are expanding their footnote disclosure by many pages, it's even harder to figure out which notes make for worthwhile reading. Sun Microsystems, for example, included 33 pages of footnotes in its 2002 10-K filing, more than 3 times the amount of footnotes it had in its 2000 report and more than 10 times its footnote disclosure in 1999.

That's frustrating for those investors who make an effort to read the footnotes, because we feel as if we're being buried in a sea of 8-point type every three months when a new filing comes out. Multiply that by even a few companies—a typical small investor might own five individual stocks—and you're talking about a few hundred pages of fine print each year.

It's not that companies relish putting all that fine print into their filings. In the mid-1990s, the SEC even considered a proposal that would have essentially eliminated the footnotes altogether. Many companies claimed that the footnotes made their annual reports too complex for individual investors to understand and appealed to the SEC to change its rules. "It's sometimes difficult for investors to get the real message," General Electric's comptroller said at the time.[3] Under that proposal, professional investors still would have had access to the information, but individuals who wanted to see the fine print would have had to ask for it. Luckily, over 1,000 investors complained loudly to the SEC, and the plan to eliminate the footnotes was defeated.[4] One could only imagine how much more serious the recent accounting scandals would have been without companies being required to provide footnote disclosure to all investors.

In light of the recent scandals, some companies have tried to make it easier for individual investors to follow along by providing additional details in the Management's Discussion and Analysis (MD&A) section of the reports or including glossaries that define company-specific finance terms. But, like it or not, the footnotes still remain the best place to find the most valuable information.

"Many of the things that companies put in their footnotes should be highlighted, instead of being buried," says Gerard Strable, an individual investor in Sarasota, Florida. Even though he's retired and has a background in finance, Strable says he finds many companies' disclosures too difficult to read. "There's too many things in there that they don't tell you about any place else."

For those investors who have never read the footnotes, finding the time to read all of this additional material is not going to be easy, particularly since it's hard to figure out exactly what to look for. Reading footnotes really is like searching for that proverbial needle in a haystack. Even investors who regularly read the fine print say they often feel as if they're missing something important.

Mel Longnecker, a retired investor who lives near Harrisburg, Pennsylvania and describes himself as detail-oriented, spent a lot of time reading Tyco's footnotes but still wound up losing money when the stock fell sharply. He bought Tyco shares after the company bought Amp, a Harrisburg-based manufacturer that Longnecker was very familiar with. "All of my reading didn't do me any good because I still got burned," says Longnecker. "I wasn't aware of anything, but then again, a lot of other very astute people got burned too."

While many companies are filling their reports with additional pages of risk factors—information that up until recently typically was provided only in a prospectus—they're not exactly posting red flags or, as some people have suggested, a skull and crossbones next to an item in the fine print. In addition, while some companies are trying to make their footnotes more accessible to average investors, the footnotes are still full of accounting-speak that makes them difficult to read. Although this may change eventually, at least for now, investors who want to read the fine print have to pick up at least a working knowledge of some of the lingo used.

Some individual investors have developed their own techniques for finding potential problems buried in the fine print. Bakul Lalla, a self-trained individual investor in Norwalk, California, has developed a 14-point checklist for evaluating companies whose stock he owns as well as the stock of companies he's considering investing in. Among the things he looks for are related party transactions and director and officer compensation, which are usually found in the proxy statement, and changes in inventory methods, revenue recognition policies, pension obligations, and short and long-term debt, disclosures typically found in the footnotes.

Even so, Lalla says he only takes about 30 minutes to review a typical 10-K the first time around and about 15 minutes on a 10-Q. If he spots some red flags, he'll go back and read the filing more closely. Still, it's a system that he's worked on perfecting since he began investing in 1986.

"Most of the gory details are usually buried in the small print," says Lalla, which is why he never skips the footnotes.

Many analysts used to advise investors to stay away from companies with epic-size footnotes. Tyco, for example, had more than 30 pages of footnotes in its 2000 10-K and 27 pages of footnotes in its 1999 report, well before extra disclosure became de rigueur. WorldCom's footnotes ran on for 49 pages in its 2000 10-K filing. The mere length of the footnotes at both of these companies probably should have served as an early warning sign that their financial statements were overly complicated, even for investors who didn't bother to read them.

"If you had the right numbers on your income statement, you didn't need as many footnotes," says Turner.

But Turner says that situation is beginning to change now as larger companies are providing more detail in an effort to show that everything is out in the open. Few people, himself included, Turner says, would argue that General Electric's additional disclosure is a negative. "Greater disclosure is good. Of course it's good that companies are doing this and telling us how they got to a particular figure."

One study by Merrill Lynch technology analyst Steve Milunovich illustrates how things have changed when it comes to footnotes. In April 2001, Milunovich looked at the size of the 2000 10-K filings by 43 technology companies and found that companies with shorter filings significantly outperformed companies that filed longer reports with the SEC. But in April 2002, when Milunovich repeated his study with the 2001 10-K filings, which were on average 36 percent larger than the crop of 2000 reports, he found that the stock of companies with larger 10-Ks outperformed those companies that had smaller reports.[5] How could investors' preferences change so quickly over the course of a year so that now investors were rewarding those companies that had more complex filings? One word: Enron.

Given the growing amount of information available, perhaps the most important thing for individual investors to keep in mind is that there's no need to play "Beat the Clock" and read the footnotes all at once. Remember: Professionals look for new pieces of information in the footnotes. The only way to find them is to compare one year to another, which is simply impossible to do quickly.

Start working through the footnotes by taking a closer look at one company that you know well, or think you know well, and highlighting items that seem important as well as those that seem confusing. What makes something important? That's also (unfortunately) subjective. As several professional investors noted in Chapter 2, different footnotes are more important for different companies. At Tyco, you'll remember, the acquisition footnote was the most important one. Another strategy that works is looking at the same footnote for the same company for two different years and highlighting any differences. This test is particularly easy to do with the significant accounting policies footnote. Chances are you'll be surprised at what you find.

Also keep in mind that if a particular footnote still is not clear, even after reading it several times, that should tell you something. Even though these footnotes usually are written in accounting-speak, most investors should be able to get a basic idea of what's going on. Still, sometimes the company is purposefully trying to complicate things, which should certainly serve as a warning sign.

It's also important not to read the footnotes in a vacuum, without looking at the financials. Some companies, including General Motors, provide helpful hints in their financials that link specific numbers to the corresponding footnote, making it easier to get the story behind the number. And the MD&A frequently provides clues on the items that management considers to be particularly important, though it will not provide details on when management is being overly aggressive with their accounting.

"If you're going to do research, you have to dig in," says Dave Halford, of Madison Investment Advisors and the Mosaic Fund Group. "There's no easy way to do this."

Colette Neuville can certainly attest to that.

CHAPTER 4

Charge It!

EACH QUARTER, COMPANIES announce billions and billions of dollars in charges that investors are told to ignore because they're described as one time, or nonrecurring, or unusual, or some other word meant to conjure up a unique set of circumstances that can only take place when Jupiter aligns with Mars. Even when the next quarter or next year rolls around and the same company announces another set of suspiciously similar charges, few people—analysts, financial journalists, and especially individual investors—stop to question whether it's really appropriate to treat these expenses as one-time events.

The charges themselves have a broad range of names—everything from asset markdowns to merger-related expenses to restructuring charges. And unlike other numbers that require investors to dig through the fine print, companies often tout these "special" charges when they first report their quarterly results. The idea behind this is for investors to think about the company's earnings *as if* these pesky charges simply didn't exist.

In their quarterly earnings releases, companies typically describe this as pro forma earnings or operating earnings, names that have no specific meaning and that give companies lots of flexibility to present their earnings in the best possible light.* While operating earnings often can be a more useful tool than net income in evaluating a company's future performance, the lack of rules has prompted many companies to take an overly broad approach when it comes to counting routine expenses as "special" items.

"There's 10 different ways to define operating earnings. It's a little like a recipe," says Bruce Gulliver, chief investment officer for Jefferson Research, a boutique research firm in Portland, Oregon.

For the most part, stock analysts have played along by excluding these one-time charges from their quarterly earnings estimates, such as those provided to Thomson/First Call, which are widely available online. Business journalists have also played a role by reporting on whether a company missed or met its earnings estimates, often without fully explaining the types of expenses that have been excluded.

But we investors also bear some responsibility by focusing too much of our attention on whatever "headline number" the company feeds us in its quarterly earnings release, without bothering to check that number against those disclosed in the company's 10-Q and 10-K filings. By deducting all sorts of expenses, many companies have been able to report pro forma results in their earnings releases that are substantially better than those reported to the Securities

---

* It's pretty easy for investors to confuse operating earnings with operating income, but the terms don't mean the same thing. Operating earnings is a pro forma number that subtracts some costs and expenses from net income but doesn't exclude others. What's included and excluded can change from quarter to quarter or year to year, which is why this "number" is talked about only in quarterly press releases and never in the company's SEC filings.

and Exchange Commission (SEC) several weeks later, when few of us are still paying attention.

A new SEC rule—Regulation G—which went into effect in March 2003, makes it a lot easier for investors to see the difference between the two numbers. Under this new rule, companies that report pro forma earnings to investors are also required to explain how (and why) the number differs from net income as defined by generally accepted accounting principles (GAAP). Even before the new rule went into effect, many companies began touting their GAAP results in press releases, in an effort to reassure investors who had grown wary of pro forma results. Of course, it's important to remember that GAAP still gives companies a great deal of lee-way because under the accounting rules, companies need to make all sorts of choices that can have a huge impact on the bottom line. (For more on this, see Chapter 2.) As a result, even companies that tout GAAP numbers in their earnings reports may still be making aggressive accounting assumptions—information that's really dis-cernable only by reading footnotes in the 10-Qs and 10-Ks.

SEARCH TIP

When it comes to quarterly earnings releases, most companies try to focus investor attention on the good news, such as their pro forma earnings, before segueing into GAAP net income, which is almost always lower. The truth—or at least the most interesting number—usually lies somewhere between the two, which is why it's important to pay close attention to the special charges. Compare both the pro forma and GAAP results side by side—something that's much easier thanks to the SEC's new Regulation G. If there's a big dif-ference between the two numbers, it pays to dig a bit deeper and poke through the footnotes for more details on these charges.

New rules were needed because during the late 1990s, pro forma reporting had become endemic. The problem was so pronounced that in December 2001, the SEC even issued a highly unusual warning to investors to treat pro forma earnings with suspicion because they "might create a confusing or misleading impression."[1] In 1992, only 31 companies in the Standard and Poor's (S&P) 500 reported a one-time charge. By 1999, more than half had taken at least one special charge. By the end of 2002, only 58 companies in the S&P 500 index did *not* announce any special charges, according to Thomson Financial/Baseline. This growing use of pro forma numbers was occurring despite the SEC's December 2001 warning and at a time when accounting scandals had jangled many investors' nerves.

One of the biggest critics of this trend has been Warren Buffett. In his 2002 letter to shareholders, Buffett snidely noted that Berkshire Hathaway would "make a little history" by reporting pro forma results that were lower than the company's GAAP results—something he said no other company he knew of had done.

"If you've been a reader of financial reports in recent years, you've seen a flood of 'pro forma' earnings statements—tabulations in which managers invariably show 'earnings' far in excess of those allowed by their auditors," Buffett wrote to shareholders. "In these presentations, the CEO [chief executive officer] tells his owners 'don't count this, don't count that—just count what makes earnings fat.' Often, a forget-all-this-bad-stuff message is delivered year after year without management so much as blushing."[2]

Not too long ago, the only time that companies really talked about pro forma results was when they had merged with another company and wanted to provide investors with some basis of comparison. But sometime in the late 1990s, a few Internet companies

On January 24, 2001, Qwest Communications released what it called "record revenue and earnings," noting at the top of its earnings release that this marked the 15th consecutive quarter that the company had either met or exceeded analysts' earnings expectations. Net income, the company said, was up 44 percent for the fourth quarter to $270 million and 54 percent for the year to $995 million—impressive numbers to be sure. These same figures were repeated over and over again that day and the next in various media reports about Qwest's results. (For more on Qwest, see Appendix B.) Reporters at the two Denver newspapers, where Qwest was based, described the results as outstanding. Even *The Wall Street Journal*'s story on Qwest the next day noted how well the company was doing when compared with more traditional competitors like AT&T, Sprint, and WorldCom, companies that the article noted were struggling at the hands of more nimble competitors like Qwest.*

Investors snapped up Qwest's shares on January 25, sending the stock up by $2.44 in very heavy trading to close at $47.06. The problem, however, was that net income as reported by Qwest wasn't actually net income, a term that has a specific meaning under GAAP rules, though investors would have had to have carefully read the release to figure this out. Using the GAAP definition, Qwest's results weren't quite as spectacular as had been reported and, had they been made available to investors that day, would have painted a sharply different picture of the company. Nearly two months later, in Qwest's 10-K filing, the company reported a net loss of $116 million (vs. the $270 million in pro forma net income) for the quarter and an $81 million net loss for the year (a far cry from the $995 million in pro forma income). Yet, in the days after Qwest filed its 10-K not a single newspaper noted the discrepancy between the two sets of numbers.

---

* "Qwest Net Soared, Up 44% on Strong Sales of Services," *The Wall Street Journal*, January 25, 2001, p. B6.

began deducting various expenses that they considered to be extraordinary—Amazon.com regularly deducted its marketing expenses, for example, descrbing them as unusual expenses— enabling many companies to report substantially better pro forma results than they otherwise would have had they used GAAP rules. As more and more companies began to realize that investors didn't seem to mind the pro forma results—remember, ignorance was bliss—and were even rewarding companies based on these rosier results, many more decided that it made sense for them to report results in this way too.

> ## RED FLAG
>
> Look carefully at companies that report big differences between their pro forma earnings and net income. Ask yourself what the reason is for the gap and try to determine what expenses are being excluded.

Given investors' reactions to rosier pro forma results, some companies began excluding special charges quarter after quarter, assuming—correctly, it turns out—that few people would notice a pattern. Even when the charges were huge or were taken repeatedly and for the same or similar-sounding reasons, few people seemed to ask questions.

For example, Cendant Corp., a New Jersey–based consumer services company whose brands include Avis, Days Inn, and Jackson Hewitt tax preparation services, took 20 special charges—one for each quarter—between January 1998 and December 2002, according to Reuters Information Network. That was more than any other company during that period and seems more than a bit brazen, given Cendant's history of aggressive accounting. During that time, these "special" charges added up to nearly $5 billion, according to Reuters. Other companies that have consistently taken one-time charges according to Reuters include Cardinal Health, HCA, Kroger, Motorola, and Yahoo! (See Exhibit 4.1.)

RED FLAG

Be wary of companies that seem to take "special" charges quarter after quarter or year after year.

Why would any company want to repeatedly announce big charges? Because as long as everyone was happily ignoring these charges, it was easy for companies to brush away all sorts of bad decision making. Not only were these charges able to help the companies exceed earnings expectations and enhance important valuation ratios, such as their price to earnings ratio (P/E) for the current quarter or period, but they also laid the groundwork that would enable companies to make future earnings look better as well. Individual investors, however, don't fare as well because the various charges make it much more difficult for us to figure out what's really going on.

"The economy was deteriorating and companies didn't want to report poor earnings," says Mitch Zacks, president of Zacks Investment Research, which, like Reuters, began tracking these special charges at the request of large institutional investors who have begun to pay a lot more attention. "Big institutional investors knew what was going on, how Motorola and the other companies were constantly able to beat their earnings expectations. But small investors really got burned by this because they didn't come to the table with this history."

EXHIBIT 4.1

Something Special's in the Air

The listed companies repeatedly took "special" charges or gains during the 20 consecutive quarters between 1998 and 2002. Investors and most Wall Street analysts have long ignored such "special" situations when calculating earnings because the items were considered to be nonrecurring. But some companies seem to take nonrecurring charges (or gains) pretty regularly, including the six companies at the top of this list, which had a "special" charge or income every single quarter over the five-year period.

Company	# of Quarterly Charges/Gains	Company	# of Quarterly Charges/Gains
Cendant	20	Albertsons	18
Eastman Kodak	20	AT&T	18
Edison International	20	BMC Software	18
EOG Resources	20	Dana	18
Harrahs Entertainment	20	Du Pont De Nemours	18
HCA	20	International Paper	18
Weyerhauser	20		
		Goodrich	17
Cardinal Health	19	Ryder System	17
Costco Wholesale	19	Sun Microsystems	17
Kroger	19		
Newell Rubbermaid	19		
Thermo Electron	19		
TMP Worldwide	19		
Tyco International	19		
Waste Management	19		

Source: Reuters Information Network.

Consumer products giant Procter & Gamble (P&G), for example, launched a large restructuring plan in July 1999 and proceeded to take restructuring charges, which the company described to investors as "one-time" items, through June 2003. Over those four years, the company took an estimated $3.6 billion in restructuring charges, or about $900 million each year, creating a significant gap between net income and the "core earnings" that P&G, analysts, and the media tended to focus on. In December 2002 P&G said that it would stop reporting two sets of numbers at the start of its fiscal year in July 2003.[3]

Not only do big charges make future earnings look better because most investors simply focus on the absolute change between the two numbers, but companies sometimes wind up reversing a part of that charge at some point in the future, which also boosts earnings. One simple way to think about this is how you feel after finding a $20 bill that you thought you had lost stuffed deep in a pocket somewhere. You feel richer, even if you're not. When a company takes a big charge, the money is gone, until the chief financial officer (CFO) finds it again and turns it into earnings. Companies practically never tout these reversals—after all, it is found money—though the details usually can be found in the company's footnote on restructuring.

In a 1998 speech at New York University called "The Numbers Game," former SEC chairman Arthur Levitt warned that the SEC had begun to notice a pattern of companies taking large restructuring charges, only to reverse a portion of these charges later on, creating earnings. In the speech, Levitt warned investors to pay attention to large restructuring charges. But few investors, including many large institutional players, heeded his call. "Why are companies tempted to overstate these charges? When earnings take a major hit, the theory goes, Wall Street will look beyond a one-time loss and focus only on future earnings. And if these charges are conservatively estimated with a little extra cushioning, that so-called conservative estimate is miraculously reborn as income when estimates change or future earnings fall short."[4]

Recently the SEC has begun to focus a lot more attention on companies that take big charges, particularly those that have done so repeatedly. In a November 2002 speech to members of Financial Executives International, a group largely comprised of CFOs, SEC commissioner Cynthia A. Glassman compared this practice to a football team constantly coming up with new and ever-more creative reasons on why they lost an important game. "The clever ones always take different one-time charges," Glassman told the group.[5]

In March 2003, as part of the new rules required by Sarbanes-Oxley—federal legislation passed in July 2002 that was designed to reign in corporate fraud—the SEC introduced a rule that is already putting the corporate creativity Glassman described to the test. Under the new rule, companies can no longer take a one-time charge when there's a reasonable likelihood that they will need to take a similar charge within the next two years or if they have done so within the previous two years. The rule was established to prevent some of the abuses that took place at both Tyco and WorldCom, companies known as serial acquirers because much of their business strategy was based on buying other companies. Immediately following the acquisitions, Tyco and WorldCom would take large restructuring write-offs—charges that sometimes even exceeded the purchase price of the companies acquired. Then the process would be repeated after the next acquisition, with investors once again told to ignore the charges.

"We are concerned when a company takes a restructuring charge year after year and keeps trying to eliminate it from earnings by telling investors they [the charges] are special or otherwise irrelevant," says Carol Stanley, chief accountant for the SEC's Corporation Finance Division.[6]

It's unclear exactly how the new rule will work for other serial acquirers going forward. The SEC says it will be keeping a close eye on special charges from now on and doesn't see how any company— including serial acquirers—can get around the new rules, which essentially create a four-year buffer zone. Still, it seems perfectly plausible that companies can come up with slightly different names for what are essentially restructuring or merger-related charges, in the hopes of flying under the SEC radar. (See Exhibit 4.2.)

EXHIBIT 4.2

Calling All Charges

Here are some of the names companies used to describe one-time or special charges in 2002.

Acquisition charge	Nonrecurring charge
Amortization of intangibles	Research and development charge
Asset sale loss	
Closing costs	Restructuring charge
Foreign exchange loss	September 11 charge
Goodwill amortization	Severance charge
Impairment charge	Start-up costs
Insurance settlement	Stock compensation
Investment loss	Tax adjustment loss
Litigation charge	Workforce-related charge
Merger charge	Write-down
Noncash charge	Write-off

Source: Thomson Financial/Baseline.

Companies that routinely take write-offs and present pro forma results say that they're simply trying to provide investors with a more accurate view of their company. A spokesman at Motorola, for example, defended its seemingly routine practice of taking special charges as "not related to the core activities of the Company; are of an unusual nature or are items that are not expected to recur."[7]

Among the most vocal critics of the return to GAAP reporting now mandated by the SEC has been T. J. Rodgers, chief executive of Cypress Semiconductor in San Jose. Rodgers has frequently said that GAAP actually means government's arbitrary accounting principles."I'll be damned if I'll let accountants take Cypress's real and hard-earned profits away from our financial report card with phony losses," he said in a speech at Stanford University in June 2002.[8]

At a company like Cypress, the difference between pro forma and GAAP results can be substantial, even without any changes to the rules on options that the Financial Accounting Standards Board (FASB) began considering in early 2003 (changes Rodgers also opposes). (For more on options, see Chapter 5.) In 2002 Cypress lost $249.1 million, or $2.03 a share under GAAP, compared with a pro forma loss of $37 million, or 30 cents a share. In its 2002 fourth-quarter earnings release, Cypress said that it took two special charges during the quarter for $88.3 million. Though the company had taken special charges for at least the five previous quarters, it was the first time that Cypress had provided a breakdown and exact numbers for the charge.

Rodgers has repeatedly advocated the creation of a pro forma accounting standards board, "chartered to make clear, consistent corrections to the GAAP statements."[9]

The numbers behind many of these "one-time" charges are hardly spare change. In 2002 S&P 500 companies wrote off nearly $1 *trillion* in special charges, including more than $500 billion in goodwill alone, according to Valuation Research, an independent appraisal firm that works with Fortune 1000 companies. Many companies blamed the charge-offs on the stagnant economy and changes in accounting rules that essentially encouraged them to write off as much goodwill as possible.

Bankrupt telecommunications giant WorldCom alone announced in a March 2003 press release that it had taken a $79.8 billion charge, including $34.8 billion in property, equipment, and other intangible assets, in 2002. AOL Time Warner wrote off nearly $100 billion in goodwill in 2002, blaming the charge on new FASB accounting rules that went into effect at the beginning of the year. The new rules required companies to take a hard look at their assets and mark down anything that had declined in value, some-what similar to a way a department store might mark down winter boots at the end of the season.

It's not that these billions in charges were inappropriate. The new FASB goodwill rule prompted many companies to take large charges in 2002 and blame them on the accounting rule change. In addition, the economy truly was sputtering along, which forced many companies to make additional layoffs and take charges to cover severance and other restructuring costs.

However there's absolutely no reason why investors should instinctively ignore big charges, which companies almost always describe as noncash charges, particularly when a company repeat-edly takes these so-called "special" charges. Lynn Turner, the former chief of accounting at the SEC, says that a pattern of recurring charges often can serve as an early warning sign for investors, if only we bothered to pay attention.

"The companies always say it's a noncash charge," says Turner. "But when investors see that, they should see a great big red flag. What is wrong with this business? That's what investors should say. Any time management is saying it's a noncash charge, investors ought to put their hands over their pockets."

IN FOCUS

Even after some of the huge goodwill write-offs announced during 2002, S&P 500 companies still had lots of goodwill on their balance sheets—as much as $1 trillion, according to some estimates. In the past, investors tended to think of goodwill (when they thought about it at all) as an accounting place-holder on the balance sheet. In mergers, it was the difference between the actual assets of the company being acquired and the purchase price paid by the acquiring company. For example, when Hewlett-Packard acquired Compaq Computers in May 2002, nearly 60 percent of the $24.2 billion purchase price—$14.5 billion—was accounted for as goodwill.

But the sheer amount of goodwill sitting on corporate balance sheets, combined with new FASB accounting rules that require companies to test for goodwill impairment, means that it is more important than ever for investors to pay attention to goodwill. Now, when companies announce large goodwill charges, stocks tend to start falling because the charges are often viewed as signs of deeper problems, notes Alfred King, vice chairman of Valuation Research.

"So many people say that an impairment is just an accounting entry because it's a noncash charge," says King. "But any company with a significant impairment charge is really a symptom of lax management. What it really says is that someone paid too much and wasted shareholder's money."

Indeed, two different studies—one from academia and another from Thomson/Baseline, a unit of Thomson Financial, which issues First Call earnings estimates—show that companies that routinely pump up operating earnings by deducting special charges quarter after quarter make for particularly bad investments. A study conducted by Russell J. Lundholm, a professor at the University of Michigan's Business School, examined more than 120,000 quarterly earnings releases over an 11-year period and found companies that take large charges regularly tend to have lower future cash flows. The study also found that three years after the earnings announcements, those companies that took large charges had stock returns that were 45 percent lower than those companies with relatively few charges.[10]

Thomson/Baseline coined a new phrase to assess earnings for companies that take repeated charges: earnings purity. The idea is that companies with recurring special charges have earnings that are cloudier than companies that take relatively few charges.

In a study by Thomson/Baseline analysts, companies that took lots of charges—those that would not report *any* operating earnings without first deducting the charges—were assigned a purity score of zero and performed much worse than companies whose operating earnings were write-off free. Those companies received a score of 100. Between June 2001 and December 2002, those with 100 percent earnings purity saw their stocks decline nearly 8 percent, while those companies with zero earnings purity saw their stocks decline by 34 percent. During that same 18-month period, the S&P 500 index declined by 26.4 percent, meaning that investors who avoided companies with recurring "special" charges would have fared better.[11]

"The study found that, contrary to popular opinion, these charges matter," says Ronald Perez, a vice president at Thomson/Baseline who worked on the study. "Investors want to buy companies where earnings are growing, but if the company is only growing through financial engineering and one-time gimmicks, then it's not really growing."

Many analysts as well as some journalists have begun to take a much more critical look at these recurring charges. In September 2002, analysts at Bear Stearns & Co. issued a hefty report that took an industry-by-industry look at how some companies repeatedly used unusual charges to pump up earnings. The study found that even companies in the same industry often took very different approaches when it came to special charges. For example, some advertising firms excluded severance and restructuring charges from pro forma earnings while others counted those expenses against income.

"Readers of earnings releases and financial reports need to maintain a healthy skepticism and accept no statement at face value," the Bear Stearns report warned. "Since [pro forma] earnings are almost always higher than the reported GAAP numbers, there has always been some skepticism within the investment community about management's motivation."[12]

Some analysts now believe that *any* company that takes more than eight "special" charges in any 12 quarters probably should be avoided, or at least given a careful once-over. But investors with a low tolerance for risk may want to set the bar even lower. Even over shorter periods, the Thomson/Baseline study found that companies that took repeated charges fared worse than those that didn't.

While the new SEC rules on pro forma earnings and "special" charges make it harder for companies to engage in this type of earnings subterfuge, it doesn't make it impossible. As SEC Commissioner Glassman noted in her speech to CFOs in November 2002, some companies have already become increasingly creative with the names they're using to describe these special charges.

As investors, we need to start viewing all of the fancy names companies call these "special" charges with a hefty dose of skepticism and think carefully about what the company is trying to say. Sometimes charges really are necessary and even though we shouldn't ignore them, it's okay to exclude them from the income statement without raising the Enron alarm. Still, many times, these charges are just another way for company executives to pull the wool over our eyes.

CHAPTER 5

Optional Illusions

HOW CAN A COMPANY report a profit when it otherwise would have reported a loss? Simple: by using a perfectly legal accounting trick that enables a company to pretend it costs absolutely nothing to hand its employees millions of dollars' worth of stock options each year.

In 2001 Eastman Kodak reported a profit of $76 million, or 26 cents a share. But Kodak, a component of the Dow 30, would have reported a $3 million loss—a penny a share—if the accounting rules required it to account for its options as an expense.[1] Yet only investors who flipped to the footnotes in Kodak's 2001 10-K filing would have realized this.*

---

* Kodak's disclosure on options in its 2002 10-K provides a perfect example of why investors really need to read these documents carefully to avoid falling for the company line. In its 2002 10-K, Kodak says that once option expenses were accounted for, it would have made $2 million, or a penny a share, in 2001. But in its 2001 10-K, Kodak says it would have lost $3 million, or a penny a share, after options expenses for that same year. How could the company report two different

67

Kodak is hardly the only company benefiting from this rule. Many publicly traded companies rely on options to pump up earnings, although the practice is particularly endemic at technology companies, where options have long been a key part of employee compensation.

Few individual investors realize that while accounting rules require all companies to disclose the impact that expensing options might have on the company's bottom line, they're required to do so only in the footnotes. And up until as recently as December 31, 2002, when the Financial Accounting Standards Board (FASB) changed its rules to require quarterly disclosure, companies were required to disclose the potential impact on earnings only once a year. In this footnote, the companies describe their income (loss) after subtracting options expenses as pro forma earnings. But unlike the pro forma numbers that many companies like to tout (for more on this, see Chapter 4), these pro forma figures are almost always worse, which is why they are buried in the footnotes.

"Does anyone really give a damn about the options numbers in the footnotes?" asks Jim Leisenring, the former vice chairman of FASB, who was one of those leading the charge back in the early 1990s to change how companies account for options.

Under that proposal, companies would have been required to charge the cost of employee stock options against income. But

---

numbers for the same year without restating its numbers, which Kodak did not do? In its 2002 filing, Kodak uses net income from continuing operations. But in its 2001 filing, Kodak uses net income. FASB rules clearly state that companies are supposed to use net income in their options disclosure, but they don't explicitly prohibit a company from using net income from continuing operations. It's a subtle word change, but one that means the difference between reporting a profit and a loss and shows how a company can follow generally accepted accounting principles and still push the envelope.

many companies were vehemently opposed to the FASB proposal and lobbied heavily against it. Under intense political pressure, including an 88–9 vote by the United States Senate on a resolution urging that the proposal be dropped, FASB backed down.

To see what prompted such outrage, it helps to understand exactly what an option is and how it works. Many companies grant options to their employees and their executives as a form of compensation. An option gives the employee the ability to buy a certain number of shares from the company at a predetermined price, typically the market price for the stock on the day the option is granted. Employees usually are able to buy a certain number of shares each year at the predetermined price up until the options expire, which can be as long as 10 years.

When the company's stock is rising, the longer that the employee remains with the company, the bigger the potential for profit. Employees profit—substantially during the late 1990s—when they are able to purchase those shares from their employer at one price, say $10 a share, and then sell them on the open market at a higher price, say $30 a share.

For the companies, distributing options enables employers to save on things they'd have to spend actual cash on—such as salaries and benefits. And since companies are the ones selling their own stock, any revenue they take in from their employees shows up on the income statement under nonoperating income. In addition, employers also get a nice tax break as well because the difference between the two sales prices—$20 a share in the example just above—is a tax-deductible expense for the company.

But investors rarely fare as well from this widespread practice. Not only can options make a company appear to be more profitable than it really is, but options almost always dilute earnings. If

 SEARCH TIP

New rules now require companies to disclose their stock options expense in chart format in their note on significant accounting policies, which is usually the first or second footnote. Companies typically report four different earnings numbers in this chart. Pay particularly close attention to the pro forma diluted earnings per share and compare that to "as reported" earnings per share, which is the number companies and media outlets use most often when reporting earnings. Then dig deeper into the footnotes to find additional details on the number of shares granted and the average cost per share.

you're like most individual investors, chances are you focus on a company's earnings per share, which is net income divided by the number of outstanding shares. When the number of shares increases because a company has distributed lots of options, earnings per share decline unless management takes steps to avoid dilution by buying back shares. (See Exhibit 5.1.)

For most companies, the options expense can be substantial, so they're more than eager to bury it in the little-read footnotes. How substantial? In 2001, $80 billion in options expenses were disclosed in the footnotes for the companies in the S&P 500, up from $38 billion in 1999, reducing 2001 earnings by approximately 20 percent compared to reported earnings. The top 10 companies in terms of options expense—all technology companies—accounted for $20.85 billion, or just over a quarter of the pro forma expenses reported by the S&P 500 companies in 2001, according to an analysis by Bear Stearns.[2] (See Exhibit 5.2.)

EXHIBIT 5.1

Real Cost of Options

IBM reported earnings for 2002 of $2.10. But factoring in the cost of options and accounting for shareholder dilution lowered Big Blue's earnings to $1.39.

(dollars in millions except per share amounts)

For the Year Ended December 31:	2002	2001	2000
Net income applicable to common stockholders, as reported	$ 3,579	$ 7,713	$ 8,073
Add: Stock-based employee compensation expense included in reported net income, net of related tax effects	112	104	82
Deduct: Total stock-based employee compensation expense determined under fair value method for all awards, net of related tax effects	1,315	1,343	972
Pro forma net income	$ 2,376	$ 6,474	$ 7,183
Earnings per share:			
Basic—as reported	$ 2.10	$ 4.45	$ 4.58
Basic—pro forma	$ 1.40	$ 3.74	$ 4.07
Assuming dilution—as reported	$ 2.06	$ 4.35	$ 4.44
Assuming dilution—pro forma	$ 1.39	$ 3.69	$ 3.99

The pro forma amounts that are disclosed in accordance with SFAS No. 123 reflect the portion of the estimated fair value of awards that was earned for the years ended December 31, 2002, 2001 and 2000.

Source: IBM 2002 10-K, p. 72.

IN FOCUS

Figuring out how a company values its options requires quite a bit of math and probably isn't worth the time for most investors. But by skimming the options footnote, investors can get a good idea about how forthcoming the company is.

Most companies use the Black-Scholes method for valuing options. This formula requires companies to make several assumptions, including how long the company expects employees to wait before exercising the option (in the fine print, this is called "the life of the option") and how much the stock price will fluctuate during that time ("expected volatility").

Unfortunately, some companies' disclosures about this expense— even buried in the footnotes—leaves much to be desired, according to an analysis by Bear Stearns. In reviewing the options footnotes for the companies in the Standards and Poor (S&P) 500, accounting analyst Pat McConnell said she found a large variation in the quality of the options disclosure and that some disclosures were presented in a way that made them "virtually meaningless" to investors.

For example, in Bank One's 10-K for 2001, the Chicago-based banking giant gave such broad ranges for how it arrived at its options expenses that investors would have been hard-pressed to duplicate the results, even if they wanted to try. Here's a sample from Bank One's footnote on options:

> The following assumptions were used to determine the Black-Scholes weighted-average grant date fair value of stock option awards and conversions in 2001, 2000, and 1999: (1) expected dividend yields ranged from 2.29%–4.86%, (2) expected volatility ranged from 19.11%–42.29%, (3) risk-free interest rates ranged from 4.85%–6.43% (4) expected lives ranged from 2 to 13 years.

According to McConnell's analysis, an option that used all of the lower assumptions (dividend yield of 2.29 percent, volatility of 19.11 percent, interest rate of 4.85 percent, and a two-year life) would be

IN FOCUS *(CONTINUED)*

worth 166 percent less than one that used all of the higher assumptions, using the Black-Scholes options pricing model. And because an investor would be unable to determine the value of those options from the information provided, it would be very difficult to get a good handle on exactly what Bank One's stock option expense adds up to. In its footnote, however, Bank One gives its pro forma options expense as $70 million for 2001.

Compare the Bank One note with the one Microsoft provided in its 10-K for the fiscal year ended June 30, 2002. Microsoft, which in fiscal year 2001 spent $3.4 billion on options—more than any other company (see Exhibit 5.2)—gives the exact numbers in each year used to determine its pro-forma options expense, making its footnote on options among the best, McConnell says.

> The weighted average Black-Scholes value of options granted under the stock option plans for 2000, 2001, and 2002 was $33.67, $29.31, and $31.57. Value was estimated using a weighted average expected life of 6.2 years in 2000, 6.4 years in 2001, and 7 years in 2002, no dividends, volatility of .33 in 2000, .39 in 2001, and .39 in 2002, and risk free interest rates of 6.2%, 5.3%, and 5.4% in 2000, 2001, and 2002.

Even if you never plan to do the calculations yourself, it should make you think twice about investing in companies that can't seem to provide this information in a way that's clear and easy to understand. Indeed, many pros, including those who normally don't pay much attention to options expenses, consider muddled disclosure to be a troubling sign for investors.

During the late 1990s, when options mania was sweeping the country and companies were distributing millions of options as part of employee compensation packages, very few investors realized that one of the reasons for those glowing results, or at least less severe losses, were options.

For example, an investor in Yahoo!, the large Internet services company, might have read that the company made $70.7 million, or 13 cents a share, in 2000, earnings that helped to illustrate that despite the massive decline in most Internet stocks that year, Yahoo! was one of the survivors. But in Yahoo's 10-K filing several months later, buried in footnote No. 8, the company noted that had it been required to expense those options, Yahoo!'s loss would have been $1.26 billion, or $2.30 cents a share. In 2001, the impact of options made Yahoo!'s loss seem much less severe. For that year, the company reported a $92.8 million loss, or 16 cents a share. But had it expensed those options, Yahoo! would have reported a loss of $983.2 million or $1.73 a share.[3]

EXHIBIT 5.2

Value of Options

*Here are 10 companies (ranked in order of pro forma expense)
that reported the largest pro forma options expense in 2001 and
the impact that spending would have had on their earnings per
share (EPS).*

Company	Pro Forma Pretax Stock Compensation (in millions)	Diluted EPS (loss) Reported	Diluted Pro Forma EPS (loss)
Microsoft*	$3,377	1.38	0.97
Cisco Systems†	$2,818	(0.14)	(0.38)
Nortel Networks	$2,743	(7.62)	(8.14)
AOL Time Warner	$2,385	(1.11)	(1.43)
IBM	$2,065	4.35	3.69
Intel	$1,728	0.19	0.04
Lucent†	$1,623	(4.18)	(4.46)
Yahoo	$1,484	(0.16)	(1.73)
Merrill Lynch	$1,423	0.57	(0.38)
Siebel Systems	$1,203	0.49	(1.02)

Source: Bear Stearns & Co.

* Fiscal year ending 6/01.
† Fiscal year ending 7/01.
‡ Fiscal year ending 9/01.

"The options have not received the scrutiny they would have if they had been in the income statement," laments Leisenring. "Disclosure is not a substitute. This needs to be recognized in the statement."

Not expensing options, Leisenring says, is simply bad accounting. If companies had to boost salaries by 10 percent, instead of handing out options to their employees as a part of compensation, that salary increase would show up in the companies' income statements as an expense.

Over the past few years, the chorus of voices raising concerns over options has grown louder. Everyone from Warren Buffett to Federal Reserve Chairman Alan Greenspan to former Securities and Exchange Commission (SEC) Chairman Arthur Levitt has said that the rules need to change. Indeed, Levitt, who was widely recognized as being a strong advocate for individual investors during his tenure at the SEC, said that his decision not to stand up for FASB in 1994 when it moved to change the rules was the "single biggest mistake" he made as SEC chairman.[4]

Buffett, in his 1998 annual letter to shareholders, asked these three rhetorical questions about options: "If options aren't a form of compensation, what are they? If compensation isn't an expense, what is it? And if expenses shouldn't go into the calculation of earnings, where in the world should they go?"[5] In his March 2003 annual letter to shareholders, Buffett used even stronger words to describe the problem with options. "With the Senate in its pocket and the SEC outgunned, corporate America knew that it was now boss when it came to accounting. With that, a new era of anything-goes earnings reports—blessed and, in some cases, encouraged by big-name auditors—was launched. The licentious behavior that followed quickly became an air pump for The Great Bubble."[6]

During the summer of 2002, concern began mounting over whether the options accounting rule was misleading to average investors. In August alone, 57 companies—almost two a day—announced that they would take options accounting out of the footnotes and onto their income statements by voluntarily agreeing to expense their options.

Despite this, the overwhelming majority—about 15,000 publicly traded companies—treat options as a freebie and are likely to continue doing so unless FASB decides to change the accounting rules on options, something it said in March 2003 that it would consider once again. Just as in 1994, people quickly began lining up to choose sides. Several weeks after FASB said it would reopen the issue, two California congressmen introduced legislation in the House of Representatives that would put mandatory expensing on hold for at least three years.[7] Similar legislation was introduced in the Senate in April 2003 by Senator Barbara Boxer (D-Calif.) and Senator John Ensign (R-Nevada).[8]

Individual investors also began diving into the options debate in 2002 and 2003 by sponsoring dozens of shareholder resolutions that would require companies to seek shareholder permission if they chose not to expense their options. For example, the National Automatic Sprinkler Industry Pension Plan sponsored a resolution at IBM's 2003 annual meeting that would have required the company to expense options for IBM executives, and won 47 percent of the shareholder vote despite the opposition of IBM's board of directors.[9]

In the past, the SEC had often ruled that such proposals were considered internal corporate business, which allowed companies to ignore similar shareholder proposals. But in late 2002, the SEC began reversing its thinking and said that companies could no longer ignore such shareholder proposals.

Those opposed to expensing options argue that many businesses, particularly start-ups and high-tech companies, would not be able

IN FOCUS

When FASB proposed a new rule on June 30, 1993 that would have required companies to account for stock options as an expense, FASB board members fully expected some companies to balk over the proposal. But they weren't prepared for the 18-month firestorm that followed, said Jim Leisenring, FASB's vice chairman at the time. "We expected it to be unpopular, but we didn't expect them to convince Congress to enact bad public policy."

Soon members of both houses of Congress, led by Senator Joseph Lieberman (D-CT) in the Senate, had introduced legislation that essentially blocked FASB from enacting the rule, even though FASB, which is an independent board, is only tangentially subject to congressional oversight.

Top technology company executives went to Washington to lobby and to testify before Congress. "There is more at stake here than the sanctity of accounting principles. Our growth—indeed our very existence—would not have occurred without the people we attracted with stock options," said Robert Gilbertson, former chairman of the American Electronics Association, a trade association, in testimony before the Senate Subcommittee on Securities on October 21, 1993. And in Silicon Valley, a demonstration called the "Rally in the Valley" drew thousands of protesters, many of them wearing STOP FASB T-shirts.

FASB, which normally works in near obscurity from its offices in Norwalk, Connecticut, didn't know what to do. Leisenring estimates that those opposed to the options rule spent more than $70 million fighting the board. On December 14, 1994, FASB announced that it was dropping its proposal and that instead, companies would be required to disclose their options expense in the footnotes to their SEC filings. FASB also said that companies could voluntarily expense their options—something that only two companies in the S&P 500, Boeing Corp. and Winn-Dixie—decided to do.

"This was one of the most vociferous and vitriolic responses that we had ever seen," Leisenring said. "Everyone ceased to support us. We could count on one or two hands the number of supporters including Warren Buffett and Sen. [Carl] Levin [D-Mich.]. We didn't have the chair of the SEC, the Senate voted 88–9 against this and there was obvious interference from the White House and the Treasury. It would have taken a lot of money to win this one."

On March 12, 2003, FASB voted unanimously to begin looking at ways to require companies to begin expensing their options by 2004, prompting 12 senators, led once again by Senator Lieberman, to voice their dissent. On the other side of the issue are Senator Levin and Senator John McCain [R-AZ], who believe investors deserve honest results. After nearly 10 years and numerous accounting scandals, this is one rematch that should be interesting to watch.

to retain employees without them. Options, they say, provide a powerful incentive to employees and align employee interests with those of shareholders.

"Why do you think they [employees] are so motivated? The answer is because they are shareholders of the company. Why are they willing to stay as late as they're staying? Why do they ride coach everywhere they go? It's because they're spending the money as if it were their own," says Cisco Systems senior vice president of corporate finance Dennis Powell.[10]

Opponents also argue that the Black-Scholes model, which is widely used to estimate options expenses, makes them appear to be higher than they actually are, particularly for a company whose stock price fluctuates substantially or for one that issues lots of options, as many technology companies do. To estimate the cost, companies have to make all sorts of assumptions, including how many options an employee is likely to buy in a particular year and what the share price will be at that time. If FASB starts requiring that options be treated as an expense, they argue, financial results will look much worse than they actually are.

Cisco Systems, for example, which reported its first quarterly options expense in November 2002, said that its net income for the quarter would have been 60 percent lower—$250 million instead of $618 million—had it been required to expense its options.[11]

"Why would we want to impose a requirement that would lead to those types of errors?" says Jeff Peck, a Washington, D.C.–based lobbyist who represents the International Employee Stock Option Coalition, a trade group made up of technology companies that are opposed to changing the existing accounting rules on options. "It will guarantee that investors get inaccurate and unreliable information."

Peck says that the coalition would prefer better disclosure of options expenses in the footnotes. Instead of presenting several charts, as is common practice in most footnotes on options, Peck says that all shareholders really need to know is what impact those options would have on earnings dilution. That, Peck says, can be explained in one or two sentences.

There's another reason why options may be worth fighting over. At some companies, options can provide a huge tax break, enabling them to save millions in taxes and, in some cases, pay no taxes, or even get a tax credit. Internal Revenue Service (IRS) rules permit a company to deduct the difference between what an option costs and its market price. For example, if an employee has an option to buy a share for $10 and then turns around and sells that share for $30, the company is able to deduct $20 from its tax bill, even though the cost of the option—the $10—never showed up as an expense on the company's income statement. Multiply that by a few million options and the tax savings really starts to add up.

Between 1996 and 2000, Enron rang up $597 million in tax benefits just from its options alone, according to a study by Citizens for Tax Justice.[12] Many other companies, including Apple Computer Inc., Cisco Systems, and Microsoft Corp., also have managed to substantially reduce or eliminate their federal tax bills because they were able to deduct millions in options expenses. In 1999 alone, according to one study, companies saved over $20.5 billion in corporate income taxes because of employee stock options.[13]

Professional money managers have their own concerns with options. But most are much more focused on earnings dilution than on trying to attach a value to the options. Some money managers, including Robert Olstein of the Olstein Financial Alert Fund, say they pretty much ignore the number companies give as their options expense in the footnotes. For approximately 200 companies that have begun to voluntarily deduct the cost of options, Olstein simply adds the number back because he considers the expense to be misleading.

"It's a fictitious expense, so I just add it back in to their cash flow," says Olstein.

But that doesn't mean he ignores the impact of the options. Instead, when a company reports earnings, Olstein tends to focus on the diluted earnings per share number instead of the more widely reported basic earnings per share.

Almost all companies report two earnings per share numbers each quarter: basic and diluted. When employees exercise their options, it increases the company's number of outstanding shares, which, in turn, tends to impact earnings per share. So if earnings are expected to increase by, say, 10 percent a year, and exercised options increase the number of outstanding shares by 5 percent a year, earnings per share are not going to grow at 10 percent, unless management decides to buy back its shares to make up for the difference. One place to look for the impact of dilution is on the quarterly earnings release.

Professionals also keep a close eye on options because it's one of those footnotes that can speak volumes about a company's management and whether it has shareholders' best interests at heart. Is the company giving away too many options to top executives and employees? Is it quick to issue new options when existing options are underwater (cost more than the current market price)?

"You need to look at how much of the company management is giving away, because some companies are giving away huge numbers of options," says Liz Fender of TIAA-CREF.

At some companies, this giveaway has continued unabated, despite the downturn in the market. According to a study by Bear Stearns, 64 companies issued options representing 5 percent or more of outstanding shares in 2001 and 33 companies, including Apple Computer, Delta Air Lines, and Merrill Lynch & Co., had outstanding options of 20 percent or more in 2001.[14]

And, if those options are no longer worth anything to employees because the strike price (the amount the employee can purchase a share for) is higher than the market price, a growing number of companies simply swap those options for new, lower-priced ones.

IN FOCUS

You've probably heard the expression "What a difference a day makes." But did you know how that expression applies to options that are underwater? Although options were designed to provide an incentive to average employees by giving them a chance to take advantage of rising share prices, the market decline that began in March 2000 means that many options issued during the bubble quickly became worthless. To make up for that, hundreds of companies have simply waved a magic wand over the older, more expensive options and replaced them with new cheaper options. Accounting rules say that as long as the company waits more than six months to issue these new options, it is not required to treat the new options as an expense. So companies simply wait to issue the new options after six months **and a day**.

Some companies have done this several times as their stock prices continued to fall. Although the options are designed as an incentive for employees, some companies even extend the exchange program to their executives and board members, the very people who should be held accountable for the decline in the stock price. In January 2003, for example, Brocade Communications, once a high-flying Internet stock whose shares traded as high as $330 in March 2000, said it was canceling 58.1 million stock options and would replace them with 29.6 million new options in July 2003. Other former high-flying companies that have done this include Lucent Technologies and Nortel Networks. Unfortunately, the same magic wand is not available to individual investors who bought shares in a company only to watch the price of those shares sink.

In an effort to improve the information investors have on options, FASB issued a new rule on the afternoon of December 31, 2002—a time when few people were paying attention—that requires all companies to begin disclosing options expenses on a quarterly basis.[15] The new rules also require companies to present their options expenses more prominently—in the first or second footnote, where the company outlines its significant accounting policies—and in a more user-friendly chart format, something a number of companies began doing voluntarily, even before the new rules were put in place.

"We heard from a lot of users that the options information wasn't easy to discern or see and we thought this would be easier," says Patrick C. Durbin, a practice fellow at FASB who was in charge of the options project.

One of the main reasons that FASB decided to begin looking at options again was because similar rules were proposed by the International Accounting Standards Board (IASB), which sets the rules that many European companies follow. Indeed, in accounting circles, where most believe that FASB was probably still too scarred from its last attempt at changing the rules on options, the IASB's decision to move forward on options was thought to give FASB a certain level of protection.

"It certainly helps that the IASB is moving forward on this," says Fender. "And the political climate is certainly very different now than it was in the early 1990s."

Oddly enough, one of the people spearheading the IASB's efforts is none other than Jim Leisenring, the former FASB vice chairman who now sits on the IASB in London. Says Leisenring: "The whole argument over options is just political, it's not accounting."

CHAPTER 6

All in the Family

SHOULD INVESTORS CARE if some chief executive officer (CEO) has his sons on the payroll? How about if a publicly traded company is leasing property from another company controlled by the CEO's brother-in-law? What about a company that guarantees millions of dollars in loans to one of its corporate executives? Should shareholders be concerned if the company does deals with other companies that are owned by its executives or board members?

For years, the answers to these questions—and dozens of similar situations—seemed to be no. So what if a CEO was allowing the company that he ran to lend a helping hand to family members, or his board members, or fellow officers? After all, wasn't that the way that business had worked for decades?

But the spate of major accounting fiascoes at companies as diverse as Adelphia Communications, Tyco International, Health-South, and WorldCom, not to mention Enron, has prompted many investors to be a lot less blasé about these types of arrangements.

Though the details were often sketchy at best, each of these companies provided information to investors on these so-called arm's-length transactions in their Securities and Exchange Commission (SEC) filings.

Airplane and helicopter leasing, lucrative consulting contracts, generous loan programs, and real estate deals involving corporate executives, board members, and their families are some of the more common items disclosed in annual proxy statements in a section usually called "certain transactions." Increasingly, this information is being included in the 10-Ks as well, in a footnote typically called "related party transactions."*

Perhaps because related party transactions have been a major source of problems over the past few years, many companies are devoting pages in their proxies and 10-Ks to such deals. Companies that have been involved in accounting scandals before seem particularly interested in coming clean with their shareholders. Cendant, for example—which, following an SEC investigation, said it had overstated its income by $500 million in the late 1990s—devoted seven and a half pages in its 2001 10-K footnotes to related party transactions and another two pages in its proxy. Two years earlier, Cendant's related party footnote in its 10-K was one sentence referring investors to its proxy, where the disclosure was just over three pages. And Tyco International, whose former CEO

---

* If the company provides this information in both the proxy and the 10-K or 10-Q, it pays to read both because there are often differences between the two disclosures. For example, in the Related Party footnote in its 2000 annual report, Enron described Andrew Fastow as an unnamed "senior officer" who was running several off-balance sheet partnerships that were trading with Enron. But investors who also read the disclosure in the proxy would have seen Fastow's name mentioned as the general manager, which, because he was Enron's CFO, should have made investors pay closer attention to these transactions.

and chief financial officer (CFO) have been charged with looting $600 million from the company, devoted three pages to related party transactions in its 2003 proxy, compared with three paragraphs in 2000.

For the most part, this extra disclosure seeks to explain to investors why the company chose to enter into a transaction with a related party rather than an independent company. For example, Gateway Computers, the troubled personal computer maker that has been criticized repeatedly for contracting with a company controlled by its CEO to provide two airplanes for him, devoted a paragraph in its 2003 proxy to explain to shareholders why it thinks that the company is getting a good deal.

SEARCH TIP

The first place to look for related party transactions is in a company's annual proxy statement. Companies use many different words to describe these transactions, including "related party transactions," "related parties," "certain transactions," and "certain relationships," to name a few. Also be sure to look for loan guarantees for the CEO or other top officers. Although new loan guarantees were outlawed by Sarbanes-Oxley in July 2002, many companies still have existing loans on their books.

For most investors, this significant increase in related party footnotes presents a bit of a quandary. While more information is almost always better than less, in some cases companies seem to be providing so much more detail that it is more difficult for investors to identify what's really important. Did Cendant really need to provide seven and a half pages of disclosure? Are all of those deals equally important? Probably not. Still, many other companies choose to limit what they disclose, figuring that less is really more.

"Some companies get convinced by their lawyers that disclosing anything that's not absolutely necessary is going to get them sued," says Beth Young, director of special projects for The Corporate Library, the nation's leading corporate governance consulting firm. Young, who also is an attorney, wrote a report on related party transactions in November 2002 that highlighted some of the strangest disclosures she found buried in companies' proxies. (See Exhibit 6.1.)

While the Financial Accounting Standards Board's (FASB's) rule on related party transactions requires companies to inform investors of any deal that is material, or significant, companies have a good deal of leeway here. For example, both Rite Aid Corp. and Tyco International took a fairly narrow view on what they considered to be material, leaving shareholders largely in the dark. Other times, companies present the information in such a convoluted way that it's hard for investors to figure out what's really going on and who is benefiting. For example, many companies still use terms like "senior executive" or "equity-method investee" to describe a related party when it would be much clearer to use an actual name and describe the exact relationship. HealthSouth, for example, which the SEC charged in March 2003 with orchestrating a $2.5 billion accounting fraud, described about $200 million in deals with related parties—companies that HealthSouth's proxy noted were owned by "various of the company's directors and executive officers."[1]

Equally frustrating is that there's no hard-and-fast rule that investors can use to determine which related party deals are potential minefields. The companies themselves provide little guidance.

EXHIBIT 6.1

Family-Friendly Companies

Here is how some companies help family members of senior officers and directors.

Bemis Co.	Companies owned by two relatives of the CEO each sold more than $8 million in products to Bemis.
Carnival Corp.	Disclosed that the brother of its chief operating officer had been hired by Waste Management to negotiate a contract with Carnival, which generated $1.3 million for Waste Management in 2001.
Costco Wholesale Corp.	Employed two sons and the brother-in-law of the CEO, two brother-in-laws and a son of another senior executive, and several family members of two different directors.
HCA Inc.	Formed MedCap Properties and appointed son-in-law of former CEO as chief manager. In 2000, MedCap purchased for $250 million 116 medical office buildings from HCA. Medcap also received $7.9 million in lease payments from HCA.

Source: Beth Young, "My Brother-in-Law's Wife and Other Related Parties," The Corporate Library, November 2002.

After describing related party transactions in their proxies and 10-Ks, companies routinely include a line that reads: "Management believes that the terms of the transaction are similar to terms that would be negotiated with an unrelated party." Even Enron said this at the end of its infamous Footnote 16 in 1999.[2] (For text of the footnote see Exhibit 2.1.)

RED FLAG

Companies routinely describe their related party transactions as arm's-length transactions that are similar to nonrelated party deals. But that doesn't mean that investors should take the companies at their word. Be particularly wary if a public company discloses significant business with a nonpublic related party.

In its rules, FASB advises investors to think carefully about related party deals: "Transactions involving related parties cannot be presumed to be carried out on an arm's length basis. Representations about transactions with related parties, if made, shall not imply that the related party transactions were consummated on terms equivalent to those that prevail in arm's length transactions unless such representations can be substantiated."[3]

While related party transactions alone should not be the only reason to avoid buying a stock, disclosures about such transactions are one more way to evaluate management and to determine whether they are working for the company's investors or for themselves. If a company seems to have significant business deals with companies it describes as related parties and doesn't provide any justification for those deals, management is basically saying that it doesn't care what shareholders think. Companies that share details on how they arrived at a particular deal for an officer or a director show they're sensitive to concerns of self-dealing.

"Companies should put as much information as possible out there on these deals," says Paul Hodgson, a senior research associate at The Corporate Library. "They should say this is the situation, we're being open about it, and you can judge us on it."

One way to get a sense of whether the deal seems legitimate or not is to apply your own common sense: Does the deal seem legitimate, or does it smack of cronyism even if it is legal and fully disclosed? For example, a year before Enron created many of its infamous off-balance sheet partnerships that led to the company's downfall, it noted in its proxy that a travel agency co-owned by Sharon Lay, a sister of Enron chairman Ken Lay, received $2.5 million in commissions for booking tickets for Enron employees.[4] In 1999, WorldCom paid $270,348 to a subsidiary of Raytheon Corp. to provide air transportation to WorldCom chairman, Bert C. Roberts. That sounds somewhat reasonable until you read the next sentence in the proxy: Raytheon leased the aircraft from a charter company owned by Roberts.[5]

Would things have turned out differently for Enron and WorldCom—and their investors—if anyone had bothered to question either company on these relatively small deals? We'll never know, of course. What we do know is that many of the companies that have been involved in financial scandals over the past few years started out disclosing relatively small related party deals that clearly benefited company executives or their families. When those deals failed to raise concern among investors, executives upped the ante and moved on to the bigger, more complex deals that in many cases led to their downfall.

"One of the things that would have to happen first is that a company does a small deal, gets away with it, and sees that it's okay," says Young.

 RED FLAG

Don't automatically dismiss small related party deals as too insignificant to worry about. They could be a sign of lax management.

The self-dealing at both Adelphia and Enron are some of the reasons why many professional investors have begun paying much closer attention to related party disclosures, after years of largely ignoring them. Indeed, many pros say these transactions can be as good an indicator as any of potential problems in the future.

One value fund analyst whose company lost millions when Adelphia Communications began to collapse in March 2002 says he now spends a substantial amount of time on the related party fine print when he reads 10-Ks and proxy statements because his fund was so badly burned before.

"In retrospect, there were snippets of information in the Ks and maybe we should have asked more questions," says the value fund analyst, who did not want his name used. "We never had the level of comfort with the management that we like to have, but we thought that the value of the assets was so compelling that absent outright fraud, it was worth it. I'm not sure that the disclosures that were there would have gotten us to that point, but we've done a lot of soul-searching on that one."

Adelphia's stock declined from $20.39 to 79 cents a share in just over two months during the spring of 2002, after the company disclosed, in a footnote, that it had guaranteed $2.3 billion in loans to companies controlled by Adelphia's founder, John Rigas, and his family. Two months later, the company said in an SEC filing that Rigas-controlled companies had borrowed $3.1 billion and that there was $150 million in related party transactions between Adelphia and other family-owned companies. On July 24, 2002, the SEC arrested and charged Rigas, two of his sons, and two other Adelphia executives with orchestrating and concealing a huge corporate fraud. Among the charges was that the company had "concealed rampant self-dealing by the Rigas Family."[6]

Scanning Adelphia's proxy statements filed with the SEC between 1997 and 2001 and jotting down a few key numbers, it's not all that difficult to see a troubling pattern developing. Sure, hindsight is always 20/20. However, the proxies contained several clues that something strange was going on at the Coudersport, Pennsylvania–based company even if all of the details weren't spelled out. Indeed, a key part of the Rigas family defense is that they disclosed everything to investors in their SEC filings and that Adelphia's accountants, lawyers, and board members approved everything. "We did nothing illegal, my conscience is clear about that," says John J. Rigas.[7]

Because Adelphia disclosed many details, it provides one of the best examples of why it's important to look closely at several years of related party fine print and focus on any changes. The situation at Adelphia also shows why it often makes sense to see how other companies in the same industry handle similar disclosures. At Cablevision Systems—which, like Adelphia, was another large, family-controlled cable concern—the size and scope of related party deals was nowhere near those disclosed at Adelphia.

RED FLAG

Be wary of companies that appear to have significantly more related party transactions than similar companies in the same business.

Even back in 1997—the year before Adelphia began its aggressive expansion—the company's proxy statement had two pages of fine print labeled "Certain Transactions," which provided details of various relationships between Adelphia and other companies controlled by the Rigas family. By 2000 this disclosure had grown to four pages. Over the five-year period, the language in Adelphia's disclosures didn't change all that much, but the numbers rose dramatically. Granted, the company was growing quickly at the time, but even so, the level of borrowing probably should have caught investors' attention. Here's how Adelphia described the borrowing by Rigas-owned entities in its fiscal 1997 proxy statement:

> On an end-of-quarter basis, the largest aggregate amount of net outstanding loans and advances receivable from affiliates (directors, executive officers and five-percent shareholders) or entities they control, including John J. Rigas, Michael J. Rigas, Timothy J. Rigas, James P. Rigas, Ellen K. Rigas, Daniel R. Milliard, Dorellenic and/or the Managed Partnerships during fiscal 1997 was $36,430,000 at June 30, 1996. At March 31, 1997, such aggregate net amount was $30,798,000.

That's a lot of words to say that Adelphia was on the hook for about $31 million at the end of the company's 1997 fiscal year. What also stands out in this disclosure is that the amount of loans declined between June 30, 1996 and March 31, 1997. But the pattern that developed over the next five years was very different, even though the language used to describe these related party transactions is almost identical. By the end of 2000, these loans increased more than eight-fold. In addition, in its 1999 proxy, Adelphia disclosed for the first time that these loans were not backed by any collateral, which given the size of the loans, should have raised some significant red flags, particularly for the company's large institutional investors. (See Exhibit 6.2.)

In its proxies, Adelphia described a number of different Rigas-controlled affiliates, among them a group called the Managed

---

EXHIBIT 6.2

Family Business

A look at how money flowed between Adelphia Communications and Rigas-controlled affiliates.

Fiscal Year Ends	Loans and Advances from Affiliates	Fees and Expenses Charged to Affiliates	Fees Paid by Adelphia to Rigas Affiliates	Income on Loans to Affiliates
3/31/1997	$30.8*	$2.5	$2.6	$1.8
3/31/1998	$52.3	$2.3	$2.5	$9.9
12/31/1998†	$47.9	$2.7	$3.4	$9.6
12/31/1999	$178.6	$5.1	$11.2	$10.8
12/31/2000	$263.1	$37.6	$15.9	$40.3

Source: Adelphia Communications proxy statements, 1997 to 2001.

---

* All figures in millions.

† Adelphia changed its fiscal year to a calendar year in 1998 and numbers for that year are for a nine-month period.

Partnerships, which was buying its own cable systems separate from Adelphia, and Dorellenic, a real estate partnership owned by Adelphia's officers and also described how money moved between the different companies. Dorellenic had a pretty modest beginning. In 1997 it received $133,000 from Adelphia. By 2000 that number had climbed to $15.9 million. In its 2000 proxy, Adelphia also disclosed that it was a co-borrower on a $47.5 million loan with another Rigas-controlled entity to purchase the Buffalo Sabres hockey team.

What Adelphia failed to share with its investors, however, was that many of these related party transactions served to boost revenues

†

while moving debt off Adelphia's balance sheet. Indeed, it wasn't until March 27, 2002, that Adelphia disclosed in a footnote in its quarterly earnings release that it was on the hook for $2.3 billion in off-balance sheet loans. Adelphia stock fell nearly 20 percent that day. When federal officials arrested Rigas and two of his sons in July 2002, officials said that members of the Rigas family had misrepresented Adelphia's earnings and net income, two key measures of any company's health.

"What we never knew was the extent of borrowings by the Rigas-owned entities," said Oren Cohen, a former cable industry analyst at Merrill Lynch who had followed Adelphia for 10 years. "And we never imagined, if that number was going to be a big number, that it would be excluded from Adelphia's financial statements."[8]

One of the major reasons professional investors probably weren't unduly concerned with Adelphia's proxy disclosures was that the Rigas family kept buying Adelphia stock, which helped to instill confidence in other investors. If Adelphia's stock declined, investors knew that the Rigas family would be the biggest losers. What those investors didn't realize—and what wasn't fully disclosed in the proxies—was that the money to buy that stock was coming from loans guaranteed by Adelphia. Had this fact been disclosed earlier, it's very likely that Adelphia's large institutional investors, including the value fund analyst whose fund lost all that money on Adelphia, would have taken a much closer look at the company.

"We're taking a lot harder look at management teams," says that analyst. "The idea that assets and cash flows can win out in spite of poor management is no longer valid."

Because companies are required to disclose only "material" transactions, they have a fair amount of discretion in deciding what information they choose to provide to shareholders. What constitutes "material" is often open to interpretation, particularly at large companies, where a $1 million deal or even a $10 million deal might be considered immaterial. One of the best examples of this is Rite Aid, the drugstore chain that was a Wall Street darling in the late 1990s, before it began disclosing numerous insider deals and ended up restating its earnings three different times in 1999 and 2000.

RED FLAG

Be on the lookout for publicly traded companies that are still run like family businesses. Look for family members in senior positions or related parties that run companies doing business with the public company.

In its proxy statement filed on May 15, 1998, Rite Aid listed two related party transactions. One was a $245,262 lease for warehouse space owned by a partnership controlled by Rite Aid's chief executive, Martin L. Grass, and his father, Alex Grass, founder of the Rite Aid chain. The second was for a $1.9 million loan that the company made to Rite Aid's executive vice president for marketing—a loan that was more than four times the employee's annual salary.

The following year, when Rite Aid filed its proxy on June 4, 1999, those two paragraphs had been expanded to fill two pages, even though only a few of the items described appeared to be new. Among the new disclosures were four more real estate deals between Rite Aid and partnerships owned by members of the

Grass family and about $12 million in products that Rite Aid had purchased from companies whose investors included Grass family members. The proxy also disclosed that Martin Grass paid 51 percent of the cost of a helicopter leased by the company in exchange for unlimited private use.

A November 1998 lawsuit filed by a former Rite Aid executive that alleged numerous conflicts of interest between Rite Aid and the Grass family prompted the big increase in related party disclosures. Although Rite Aid dismissed the allegations as coming from a disgruntled former employee, *The Wall Street Journal* began looking into Grass family ties and published a front page story on January 29, 1999 that revealed numerous ties between Rite Aid and the Grass family.[9] At the time, Rite Aid stock was trading at around $50 a share.

But at Rite Aid, the sweet insider deals were apparently just the tip of the iceberg. In its 10-K filing on June 1, 1999, Rite Aid restated its financial results for 1997 and 1998 after the SEC raised concerns about the company's accounting practices. Over the next 15 months, the company restated earnings two more times, turning profits into losses. The multiple restatements prompted the stock to fall to under $5 a share. Even several years later, Rite Aid shareholders are still reeling from bad decisions made years earlier. On June 17, 2003, Rite Aid's former CEO, Martin Grass, pled guilty in federal court to two counts of conspiracy and agreed to pay a $3.5 million fine. He faces up to eight years in prison for his role in the massive accounting fraud.

Meanwhile, the disclosures about related party transactions kept growing. In its 2000 10-K filing, Rite Aid disclosed that between 1998 and 2000, the company had purchased approximately $124 million worth of merchandise from various related parties, although it provided few details on the identity of the related parties, what type of relationship there was, or even what items were purchased. The disclosure represented more than a tenfold increase over the $12 million that had been disclosed up until that point.

In its 2000 10-K, Rite Aid also disclosed for the first time that in addition to lending its marketing director $1.9 million, it also had guaranteed two additional loans to the marketing director totaling $7.5 million. One of those loans, the new disclosure said, was so the marketing director could purchase Procter & Gamble stock.

In the spring of 2000, Rite Aid purchased those loans from the banks that had made them. Its most recent disclosure on these loans, which by October 2000 stood at $8 million, indicated that it planned to sue to recoup the money.[10] But given that at least one of the loans was secured with depressed shares of Rite Aid stock—it's not clear from Rite Aid's disclosures what if anything the other two loans were secured by—it seems likely that the only thing that Rite Aid shareholders will get out of this is a hefty legal bill.

Adelphia and Rite Aid weren't the only public companies that were essentially serving as banks for their CEOs and other senior officers. In its 2001 proxy statement, WorldCom disclosed that it was on the hook for $366.5 million in loans and loan guarantees so that its former CEO, Bernard Ebbers, could purchase company stock. In its 2003 proxy statement, Tyco disclosed that its former CEO, Dennis L. Kozlowski, still owed the company $47 million. The proxy also noted that both Kozlowski and former CFO Stephen Swartz had understated $37 million in loans in fiscal 2001 and 2000 and had received an additional $43.8 million in unauthorized mortgage loans that were later forgiven.[11] In HealthSouth's

2001 proxy, the company disclosed that its CEO, Richard Scrushy, owed the company $25 million.[12]

The situation at Tyco and WorldCom prompted Congress to include a provision in the Sarbanes-Oxley Act that prohibits public companies from either making or guaranteeing new loans to company insiders for any purpose. Existing loans, however, including those used to finance stock purchases, are not subject to the new law. After years of being an open secret relegated to a few lines buried deep in the proxy statement (if disclosed at all), analysts now expect companies to provide much greater details in their proxies and 10-Ks on any outstanding loans to officers and directors. (See Exhibit 6.3.)

During the 1990s, these loans were a pretty standard perk for many executives and directors. A study by The Corporate Library at the end of 2002 found that one-third of the 1,500 largest companies in the United States had made $4.5 billion in loans to insiders, almost all of them at more favorable terms than could be obtained commercially.[13]

Often the loans were set up so as to be forgiven over a certain period of years. For example, when The Home Depot hired a new CEO in 2000, it offered him a $10 million loan in addition to a generous salary and bonus package. The loan agreement stated that each year that Robert Nardelli remained in the job, 20 percent of the loan would be forgiven. It also included an additional $3.5 million, often called a "gross-up" in proxy statements, to cover the tax impact of the loan. The loan remains in place even though by March 2003 Home Depot stock had declined more than 50 percent since Nardelli took over.

EXHIBIT 6.3

Banking on the Company

A look at the 10 largest corporate lenders in fiscal years 2000 and 2001.

Company	Amount[*]	Notes
Wachovia Corp.	$2,200	Loan balances for unspecified purposes to directors and officers, including to certain related interests, ranged from a high of approximately $2.2 billion to a low of approximately $1.4 billion.
Adelphia Communications	$263.1	To the Rigas family, including John J. Rigas the CEO. The purpose of the loans is unspecified.
WorldCom, Incorporated	$160.8	Balance in April 2002 for stock purchase/retention. All to Bernard Ebbers, former CEO. At one time he had loans and lines of credit totalling $401 million.
Tyco International Limited	$121.2	$61,690,928 to the CEO Dennis Kozlowski. Classed as "relocation" loans. All loans largely forgiven.
Comdisco, Incorporated	$109	The loans, borrowed from a commercial bank, are the personal obligation of the participants. Comdisco has agreed to guarantee repayment to the bank in the event of default by a participant.
Dominion Resources	$84.1	Stock purchase and loan program. This amount is for all officers, including the CEO.
Bear Stearns Companies	$58.8	Cash advance loans, mostly to help fund investments in private partnerships. Loan amount to all officers, including the CEO.
Masco Corporation	$54.9	Full-recourse, interest-bearing stock purchase loans guaranteed by the company. Total for all participants: $156 million. Some $26 million to CEO.
Conseco, Incorporated	$42.1	Stock purchase and interest payment loans to two vice presidents.
Rowan Companies	$37.9	For the purchase of debentures. $25,679,000 to the CEO.

Source: "My Big Fat Corporate Loan," The Corporate Library, December 2002.

* All figures in millions.

Compaq loaned its CEO, Michael D. Capellas, $5 million in 2001 to purchase Compaq stock. The loan was supposed to be forgiven after three years. However, Compaq merged with Hewlett Packard in 2002, well before the loan was set to be forgiven. Buried deep in its 10-K filing for 2002, Hewlett-Packard noted that Compaq's board had decided to forgive the loan to Capellas prior to the merger.[14] During Hewlett-Packard's 2003 annual meeting, shareholders voted in favor of a resolution that would require the company to seek shareholder permission on future severance packages for executives.[15] (For more on shareholder proposals, see Chapter 10.)

Needless to say, neither Compaq nor Home Depot, or any of the other companies, touted these deals. Only investors who carefully read the fine print in the proxy statements or the supplemental documents to the 10-Ks would have known about these loans.

"Things like this should raise a question mark with individual investors," says Paul Hodgson of The Corporate Library. "This kind of behavior says a lot about the management as a whole."

CHAPTER 7

Pensions in Wonderland

I N *ALICE'S ADVENTURES IN WONDERLAND*, Alice slides down the rabbit hole and finds that things that look familiar are not quite as they seem. That's basically the way investors should view the complex world of pension accounting: On the face of things, it all seems to make sense. It's only when investors delve a little deeper that everything truly gets confusing.

That's because ordinary accounting is turned on its head in the pension footnote. Even the Financial Accounting Standards Board (FASB), which has begun to think about ways to reform pension accounting rules, considers the current system a big confusing mess. At a meeting to discuss changes in February 2003, FASB Chairman Robert H. Herz called the existing pension rules "an accountant's concoction."[1]

For individual investors, perhaps the single most perplexing part about pension accounting is that the rules allow companies to pretend that their pension assets grew, even when those assets actually declined. That make-believe gain shows up on the income statement and can make both net and operating income look better than they actually are. In some cases, this pension income even allows companies to report profits when otherwise they would have reported losses.

Companies are able to do this by choosing their own interest rate and assuming that their pension assets have grown by that amount. Between 2000 and 2002, when markets were falling sharply, many companies assumed that their pension assets were growing by 9 percent or more, even when plan assets actually were shrinking. General Motors (GM), for example, which has the largest pension plan in the United States, assumed that its pension assets grew by 10 percent in 2002, when, in reality, the company reported that its pension assets actually fell by about 7 percent.[2]

Using a fictional interest rate is just the beginning when it comes to sorting things out in Pension-land. Equally confusing is how contributions to a company's underfunded pension plan— what happens when the pension plan obligations exceed the money the company has set aside—actually can help the company's bottom line by reducing pension expenses and lowering the company's tax burden. In addition, numbers that appear in parentheses in the pension footnote often (but not always) mean a gain. That's different from what most investors are used to, where a number in parentheses is typically a loss. As a result, figuring out whether the company is reporting a gain or a loss takes a bit of practice and some careful reading of the fine print.

When it comes to pensions, companies can boost net and operating income by either increasing pension income or lowering pension expenses. And the only way to try and figure out what a particular company is doing is to examine the pension footnote in the 10-K, since the bulk of both pension assets and pension liabilities aren't included on the balance sheet and there's nothing that requires companies to provide this information on a quarterly basis.

"Pensions are one of the biggest areas of abuse because it's just a paper profit. It has no impact on cash. It's like waving a magic wand," says Ted Oglove, who first began studying how pension plans pump up earnings in the late 1960s.

Many professional money managers have a designated pension specialist on their teams whose primary job is to pick apart a company's pension footnote and figure out to what extent it's being used to pump up income. These specialists also examine how pension issues are likely to impact future earnings and cash flow. And several large Wall Street firms routinely publish hefty reports designed to help institutional investors navigate the pension maze.

As individual investors, however, we're essentially left to navigate this confusing footnote on our own. Just try asking your broker or financial advisor about the impact pension plans might have on a

 **SEARCH TIP**

Check to see whether the pension plan is overfunded or underfunded. To do that, turn to the pension footnote and compare pension assets to pension obligations. Both are cause for concern, but for different reasons. If assets exceed obligations, the plan is overfunded, which means that pension assets are helping to pump up net income. If obligations exceed assets, the pension plan could become a potential drag on future earnings and lead to charges against shareholder equity.

company's future earnings and overall financial health. He or she might pretend, but most will not know what you're talking about.

One small piece of good news for investors is that the pension footnote is not the most confusing footnote out there. That honor belongs to the footnote that tries to explain derivatives—a footnote that even many pros, including Warren Buffett, confess often goes over their heads (whew!). And unlike derivatives, which are widely used, understanding how pension accounting works is only important at companies that offer defined benefit plans. Newer companies— generally those started after 1982—or those with large nonunion- ized workforces tend to offer 401-K plans to their employees, instead of traditional defined pension benefits that promise a fixed payment upon retirement. Approximately 140 companies in the Standard and Poor's (S&P) 500, including Dell Computers, McDonald's Corp., and Sun Microsystems, don't offer pensions.

But at many widely held companies, such as GM, General Electric, and IBM, to name a few, pensions often have a significant impact on the company's bottom line and are simply too impor- tant for anyone who owns these stocks to ignore. (See Exhibit 7.1.)

In 2002, with the stock market declining for the third straight year and interest rates at record lows, the number of underfunded plans began rising dramatically and the level of concern over pen- sion fund accounting grew to a fever pitch. Major debt rating agencies, such as Moody's and S&P's began lowering the credit rat- ings at several large companies, including GM and Ford Motors, which, like GM, also has a large underfunded plan. *Fortune* maga- zine even compared the pension problem to the horror movie *Nightmare on Elm Street.*[3]

"This one may affect investors more than anything else since the Great Depression," says Ron Ryan, CEO of Ryan Labs, an asset

---

EXHIBIT 7.1

Companies with Largest Defined Benefit Pension Plans, 2002

These 10 companies had the largest defined benefit pension plans in 2002, making the pension footnote particularly important for investors in these companies. In 2001, plan assets exceeded obligations at 8 of the 10 companies. But by 2002, plan assets exceeded obligations at only 3 companies, which are shown in boldface.

Company	Benefit Obligation	Plan Assets
General Motors	$92.2	$66.7
IBM	$64.1	$57.6
Ford Motors	$57.9	$42.3
Verizon	**$37.9**	**$38.6**
Boeing Corp.	$35.9	$28.8
GE	**$33.3**	**$37.8**
Lucent Technologies	$30.3	$28.6
SBC Communications	$26.1	$25.0
Lockheed Martin	$21.9	$17.7
AT&T	**$15.0**	**$15.6**

Source: Credit Suisse First Boston, 2002 10-K filings.

---

* All figures in billions.

---

management firm that focuses on fixed income investments. "When investors start to realize what this is going to cost Corporate America in terms of earnings, increased contributions, higher premiums, and lower bond ratings, they'll be shocked."

According to an analysis by Credit Suisse First Boston (CSFB), aggregate earnings at the companies in the S&P 500 would have dropped by a whopping 69 percent in 2001 if accounting rules required companies to report what actually happened to their pension plans instead of what they wished had happened. At 82 companies, net income would have dropped by 50 percent or more, and half of those companies—41—would have reported a net loss instead of net gain without the benefit of the fictional pension windfall, the study found. This wasn't just a hypothetical exercise; FASB's Herz has said repeatedly that he thinks companies should report their actual pension results. Many accounting experts agree.

Think about this for just a moment. Wouldn't it be nice if all investors were able to set a fictional rate of return on their investments? Then when the market declines, as it did beginning in March 2000, we could all pretend that we were still making money. But unfortunately, such fantasies are available only to CFOs of large companies with pension plans.

Even though it's easy to get lost in Pension-land, most investors looking to get a basic understanding of what's going on really only need to focus on three things:

1. Is the pension plan overfunded or underfunded?

2. Is the company's rate of return on its pension assets realistic?

3. How much is the pension plan contributing to net and operating income, and what future impact will this have on earnings?

In order to answer these questions, you'll need to flip back and forth between the company's pension footnote in the 10-K, the financial statements, and sometimes the Management's Discussion and Analysis (MD&A). Largely due to prodding by the Securities and Exchange Commission (SEC), companies are beginning to provide additional information (in more or less plain English) on their pension plans in their 10-K filings.

IS THE PLAN OVERFUNDED
OR UNDERFUNDED?

One of the easiest tests that individual investors can perform is to check whether a company's pension plan is overfunded or underfunded. To do this, you don't need to know much about pensions and the strange rules that govern them. Simply look at two numbers: the plan assets and the benefit obligation.

ASSETS > OBLIGATIONS = OVERFUNDED
OBLIGATIONS > ASSETS = UNDERFUNDED

When a plan is overfunded, there's not as much cause for concern, although investors probably want to try to figure out how much of the company's income is coming from the pension plan. We'll get into that in a moment.

An underfunded plan is a more immediate cause for concern. Federal pension laws require companies to make sure that there's enough money—around 90 percent—to cover their pension obligations. So companies that have underfunded pension plans may be required to divert cash to those plans, instead of putting the cash to other uses. Companies that can't come up with the cash have to pay a penalty to the Pension Benefit Guaranty Corp. (PBGC), a federal agency that guarantees pension benefits. Most companies try to avoid this at all costs, because the PBGC doesn't give the money back once the plans come back into compliance. Pension rules also can require some companies with underfunded plans to take a charge to equity, yet another reason why shareholders need to pay attention to this footnote.

In 2002, approximately 325 companies in the S&P 500—90 percent of the companies that offer pension plans—reported underfunded plans, up from 240 in 2001 and 118 in 2000, according to CSFB accounting analysts David Zion and Bill Carcache. As a result, companies in the S&P 500 ponied up approximately $46 billion in cash, more than three times as much as the $15 billion contributed in 2001.[4]

Of course, in Pension-land, even this additional cash infusion can be confusing because companies that have the money to pump into their pension funds get a tax break and also can book the added income at whatever rate of return they're using. At GM, for example, using its announced 10 percent return on the $4.8 billion it added to its pension funds in 2002 automatically generates an additional $482 million in operating income for the company. At IBM, which said in December 2002 that it was pumping $4.2 billion into its pension funds, the contribution was expected to add about $350 million in operating income.

Indeed, despite their big funding gaps, Pat McConnell, senior accounting analyst at Bear Stearns, says that neither GM nor IBM was required to pump additional money into their pension funds in 2002. "They get a tax deduction when they make a contribution and the earnings grow tax-free," says McConnell. Some analysts compare such contributions to individuals making extra payments on their home mortgages.

But analysts note that companies that don't have the cash to spare, including most of the major airlines, could find themselves in a cash crunch, which would impact their credit ratings and, in a worst case scenario, have the potential to send the companies into bankruptcy.

Companies whose pension obligations exceed their market capitalization are a particular cause for concern. For 2002, Credit Suisse's Zion was predicting that the pension obligations at 31 companies would exceed the company's market capitalization. At the top of the list was AMR Corp., where the pension obligation was nearly nine times greater than its market capitalization at the end of 2002.

Several analysts note that large underfunded pension plans combined with huge other postretirement benefits, primarily health insurance for retirees, were the motivating factors behind many large steel companies filing for Chapter 11 reorganization. The bankruptcy filings—at Bethlehem Steel and National Steel among others—enabled the companies to renegotiate their pension obligations. One company, LTV Corp., filed for Chapter 7 protection in December 2001, instantly wiping out pensions and health coverage for its retirees.[5] Two large airlines—United and US Air—began seeking pension concessions after both filed for Chapter 11 reorganization in 2002. And given the state of pension funding at several other large airlines, including American and Delta, analysts believe this may be an option for these carriers too.

Ratings agencies like Moody's and S&P consider pension obligations to be similar, though not identical, to debt and have begun to look at the pension fine print a lot more closely. Among those

IN FOCUS

Most of the companies that provide pensions also provide health insurance to retirees and their families. Unlike pensions, which companies are required to fund and for which they receive substantial tax breaks, these retiree health benefits are largely unfunded. But just like pensions, the accounting is basically the same and the obligations are just as real. For both obligations, only part of the expense is reflected in the balance sheet, so investors need to turn to the pension footnote to find out the details.

In the fine print, these benefits are called "other post-employee benefits," or OPEB, and they're often pretty sizable. At General Motors, postretirement obligations stood at $57.5 billion at the end of 2002, compared with $52.5 billion in 2001. But OPEB assets were only $5.8 billion for 2002, a funding level of just over 10 percent.

GM estimates that it provides postretirement benefits to around 460,000 retirees and their surviving spouses. According to *The Wall Street Journal*, GM is the largest private purchaser of healthcare in the United States. The company spends about $1,500 a year, about $690 million, just to provide prescription drugs to each of its retirees, including $55 million a year just on the heartburn drug Prilosec.* Although GM began instituting cost-saving measures in the early 1990s—salaried employees hired after 1993 can no longer get GM health insurance upon retirement, and many salaried workers pay more for their benefits—costs are still climbing as healthcare gets more sophisticated and workers live longer.

---

* "Golden Years? For GM's Retirees, It Feels Less Like Generous Motor," *The Wall Street Journal,* February 21, 2003, p. A1.

downgraded in late 2002 were GM, Ford, and Navistar International. In bankruptcy filings, pension liabilities are treated as unsecured debt.

"When you have a big pension obligation coupled with a lot of leverage on the balance sheet and the company isn't generating cash flow, that's a pretty volatile combination," says Zion.

RATING THE RATE

One of the next things individual investors should focus on is the fictional interest rate—called the expected rate of return in the fine print. This number usually appears at the very end of the pension footnote, which makes it easy to get lost in all of the other numbers. From Chapter 2, we know that many pros, including Jim Chanos and Robert Olstein, use this rate as a quick gauge to determine whether the company is being overly aggressive in its accounting. The nice thing about looking at this rate is that it provides a quick flashpoint without having to go into the nuances of pension accounting.

In 2000 and 2001, when the S&P 500 index fell 10.1 percent and 13 percent respectively, the S&P 500 companies assumed that their pension plan assets grew by an average of 9.2 percent. Companies argue that their rates reflect long-term annual returns of 10 percent for stocks and 6 percent for fixed income investments. A typical pension fund might have 65 percent of its portfolio in stocks and the remaining 35 percent in fixed income products. But in 2002, the average pension fund declined by about 8 percent, according to several analysts' estimates, creating a growing gap between expected and actual pension returns.

"The rate of return is still too high," says Olstein. "It should be 6 percent."

That's a view also held by Warren Buffett, who has repeatedly criticized companies for setting their rates too high. In 2001, he even suggested that companies with overly optimistic rates were exposing themselves to litigation for misleading investors.[6] In 2001 Buffett lowered Berkshire Hathaway's expected rate of return to 6.5 percent from 8.3 percent a year earlier. While few followed Buffett's lead, many companies began lowering their rates in 2003, in part prompted by SEC comments that it planned to take a close look at companies whose rates came in above 9 percent.

When the expected rate of return falls, the pension expense increases. Reducing the expected rate of return by 1 percent for the S&P 500 companies would cause that expense to climb by about $10 billion. Dropping the rate all the way down to 6.5 per-cent—an almost unimaginable scenario—would cause pension expense at the S&P 500 companies to rise by $30 billion, accord-ing to an analysis by CSFB.

In addition to the expected rate of return, investors also should do a quick reality check on the discount rate that companies use. The discount rate is used to calculate the pension benefit obliga-tion (PBO) and should be close to the yield on high-grade 10-year corporate bonds, which at the end of 2002 was around 6.6 per-cent. Companies don't have nearly as much flexibility with this figure as with the expected rate of return, but it still pays to take a quick look. When the discount rate falls, the pension obligation increases. Taken together with higher pension expenses because of lower rates of return, this creates a double whammy for many companies.

A SMOOTHING EFFECT ON INCOME

The reason why accounting rules allow companies to pick their own interest rate and assume that their pension funds grew by that amount is called "smoothing" in accounting-speak. In the fine print, it's often called by its proper name, FAS 87. The rule was designed to prevent a sudden shock to earnings if a company's pension assets either fell or rose sharply one year due to stock market fluctuations.

When the stock market is rising, as it was for much of the 1990s, the smoothing rule ensures that companies aren't automatically booking gains in their pension plans as income. When the market is falling, as it began doing in 2000, smoothing means that pension fund decreases don't immediately contribute to losses. Instead, both gains and losses are deferred over time using a complicated formula.

During a prolonged bull market, some of that income does turn into earnings for the company, making results look better than they really are and, in some cases (see Exhibit 7.2), enabling a company to report a profit when it otherwise would have reported a loss. But when the market declines, the artificial earnings sweetener slowly begins to disappear, which can cause companies to report lower earnings. Even though these are just accounting expenses—something companies routinely point out to make them seem less important—instead of actual cash expenses, they still can have a very real impact on earnings. In early January, for example, GM said it expected 2003 earnings to decline by 25 percent because of sharply higher pension costs.

As a result, many analysts believe that smoothing can be very deceptive to investors, particularly those who just focus on headline numbers, such as net income. The only way to figure out how much of a company's net income is coming from its pensions is to read the fine print. (See Exhibit 7.2.)

"The valuations for some companies might not have been as high if investors had focused on the fact that these were hypothetical returns," says McConnell. "Accountants shouldn't be doing smoothing. The company should report what really happened."

Even operating income, which many pros and more sophisticated investors tend to focus on more heavily because they consider it to be a more accurate number than net income, can be positively impacted by pension income. When the expected rate of return is rising, pension expenses fall, which helps operating income. (See Exhibit 7.3.) Problems begin when the expected rate of return starts to fall, as it began doing in 2000, causing pension expenses to increase.

RED FLAG

Analysts who track pension issues say investors should be concerned if 20 percent or more of operating income is coming from pension gains.

Even when pensions account for less than 20 percent of operating income, some money managers say they're still concerned, because the earnings are not real, no matter how solid they look. To figure out the true pension impact, they crunch a few numbers, deducting pension income and service costs from operating income, which eliminates the positive impact of pension income.

EXHIBIT 7.2

Nothing But Net?

Pension income accounted for 20 percent or more of the reported net income of these companies. Pension income enabled the first six listed to report net income in 2001 when they otherwise would have reported a loss. At three companies—Verizon, Meadwestvaco, and Northrup Grumman—pension income accounted for 20 percent or more of net income during each of these three years.

Company	2001	2000	1999
Raytheon	3718%	24%	2%
Lockheed Martin	291	NM	8
Verizon	204	21	21
TRW	164	26	18
Kodak	147	6	2
Whirlpool	134	17	(4)*
Meadwestvaco	99	28	48
El Paso Corp.	52	5	NM
Northrup Grumman	51	48	48
Pactiv Corp.	45	62	NM
Weyerhauser	43	15	11
Textron	38	20	2
NCR Corp.	36	45	12
ConEd	29	24	0
Boeing	21	13	4
Norfolk Southern	21	6	24
Bellsouth	20	11	8
Eaton Corp.	20	7	1
Donnelly & Sons	20	6	3

Source: Credit Suisse First Boston, "The Magic of Pension Accounting," September 2002, p. 76.

NM = not material.

* In 1999, Whirlpool reported net pension expense.

Dave Halford, a certified public accountant and equity portfolio manager for Madison Investment Partners and the Mosaic Fund Group, said that for years IBM and General Electric have been generating 5 to 10 percent of their operating income from pensions. "The only way you'd know it is to go to the footnotes," says Halford. "The company is not usually going to reference it unless they're questioned."

In 2002 and 2003, several large institutional investors as well as individual investors began pressuring companies to exclude pension income when it came to setting executive compensation. In February 2003, facing a shareholder proposal put forth by the Communications Workers of America, General Electric said it would no longer count pension income gains when calculating its executives' compensation packages. Other companies that have generated income from their pension funds, including IBM, faced similar shareholder proposals at their annual meetings during the spring of 2003.

As some companies began to reduce their pension assumptions in late 2002, analysts who follow pension issues began focusing on the impact this reduction was likely to have on future earnings. Some analysts even compared the rosy pension returns that companies had used to pump up earnings to a narcotic-like substance that would make it hard for companies to go cold turkey. Weyerhauser, for example, used an 11 percent rate of return in 2001, enabling the company to report a big pension gain, which in turn substantially helped both net and operating income. As shown in Exhibits 7.2 and 7.3, pension income accounted for 43 percent of Weyerhauser's net income in 2001 and 26 percent of operating income. Many other companies also rely on high rates. Air freight carrier FedEx assumed a 10.9 percent rate of return

---

EXHIBIT 7.3

Better Than It Seems

At these 12 companies, at least 20 percent of operating income came from pension funds in 2001, masking the company's true results. Two companies—Prudential and Allegheny—would have reported operating losses in 2001 without the benefit of their pension fund assets.

Company	2001	2000	1999
Prudential Financial	109%	30%	5%
Allegheny Technologies	102	49	51
Unisys Corp.	63	25	11
NCR Corp.	53	46	30
Meadwestvaco	41	20	46
McDermott Int'l	36	267	7
Raytheon Co	36	11	1
Northrup Grumman	34	42	36
Pactiv Corp.	28	28	27
Weyerhauser	26	11	8
Lockheed Martin	23	19	5
Boeing	20	12	4

Source: Credit Suisse First Boston, "The Magic of Pension Accounting," September 2002, p. 78.

between 1999 and 2001. Reducing the interest rate causes pension expenses to rise, which in turn causes earnings to fall.

According to the CSFB study, 337 companies in the S&P 500 were expected to have higher pension expenses in 2003 than in 2002. At GM, for example, pension expenses were projected to increase by $2.2 billion between 2002 and 2003 based on an 8.5 percent return. (GM said during a conference call on January 9,

IN FOCUS

Almost overnight, large investors began clamoring for more information on pension plans. As a result, many companies, including those whose pension stories weren't particularly pretty, began providing many more details about this little-understood accounting issue.

Continental Airlines' 2002 10-K filing, for example, wasn't exactly brimming with good news on pensions, and the news was certainly worse than it was in the company's 2001 filing. But unlike in 2001, where the company included one vaguely worded paragraph on pension issues in its MD&A, the company devoted a full page to the subject in its 2002 10-K filing. The company even provided information that it wasn't required to, such as the asset allocation in its pension fund and what impact lowering the interest rate might have on plan assets and obligations. (See Exhibit 7.4.)

As at most major airlines, pensions are a significant item at Continental. And the sharp decline in pension assets and lower interest rates couldn't have come at a worse time, with so many airlines cash-strapped in the wake of the September 11 terrorist attacks, not to mention the sluggish economy and a war in Iraq. To find out just how serious Continental's pension problems are, investors need to look at the company's pension footnote as well as its income statement and the MD&A.

The first indication of pension problems comes on page 21 of Continental's 10-K, where the company talks about its risk factors. In this section, Continental notes that it had to reduce stockholders' equity by $250 million—never a good sign for shareholders—because of falling interest rates and decreases in its pension assets. While the company says this did not impact 2002 earnings, pension plan funding requirements, or debt covenants, it goes on to say that pension expense is expected to increase by 76 percent in 2003 to $326 million. Doing a quick per-share calculation, that works out to just over $5 per share. The company also notes that it

IN FOCUS *(CONTINUED)*

contributed $150 million in cash to its pension plans in 2002 using proceeds from an initial public offering of Continental Express. That cash infusion is likely to help 2003 earnings because the $150 million will grow at the expected 9 percent rate of return, adding about $13.5 million to operating income. In 2003, the company says that it expects to contribute another $141 million, though it does not say where that money will come from, something that investors in the company need to keep an eye on.

Several pages later, the company says that its pension plan assets shrank by 9.4 percent in 2002 (as opposed to the 9.5 percent expected return) to $866 million and that pension obligations climbed by 76 percent, or $1.2 billion. A quick comparison of assets to obligations shows that Continental's pension plans were only around 42 percent funded at the end of 2002, another troublesome sign for shareholders. Although the company doesn't say when it will be required to close the gap under federal pension rules, the sheer size of the underfunding is likely to be a problem for years to come. In this same section, Continental also discloses its asset mixture to help investors understand how it arrived at its 9 percent expected rate of return for 2002. Companies are not required to do this, but many analysts say it makes pension assumptions easier to understand. In its final word on pensions, Continental says that the difference between its expected rate of return and its actual rate of return will lead to higher pension expenses (and thus lower earnings) between 2003 and 2005.

While the improved disclosure doesn't make Continental's pension problems any less serious, it does help investors feel a bit more confident that the company is taking the problem seriously and encouraging that its shareholders do the same.

EXHIBIT 7.4

Excerpts from Continental Airlines 2002 10-K

- As a result of continuing declines in interest rates and the market value of our defined benefit pension plans' assets, we were required to increase the minimum pension liability and reduce stockholders' equity at December 31, 2002 by $250 million. This adjustment did not impact current earnings, the actual funding requirements of the plans, or our compliance with debt covenants. However, because of the decline in interest rates and the market value of the plans' assets, we anticipate that pension expense and required pension contributions will increase in 2003. Pension expense for the year 2002 was approximately $185 million. Pension expense for 2003 is expected to be approximately $326 million. We contributed $150 million of cash to our pension plans in 2002 and expect our cash contribution to our pension plans to be $141 million in 2003.

- We account for our defined benefit pension plans using Statement of Financial Accounting Standards 87, "Employer's Accounting for Pensions" ("SFAS 87"). Under SFAS 87, pension expense is recognized on an accrual basis over employees' approximate service periods. Pension expense calculated under SFAS 87 is generally independent of funding decisions or requirements. We recognized expense for our defined benefit pension plans of $185 million, $127 million, and $124 million in 2002, 2001 and 2000, respectively. We expect our pension expense to be approximately $326 million in 2003.

The fair value of our plan assets decreased from $956 million at December 31, 2001 to $866 million at December 31, 2002. Lower

---

EXHIBIT 7.4 *(CONTINUED)*

investment returns, benefit payments and declining discount rates have increased our plans' under-funded status from $587 million at December 31, 2001 to $1.2 billion at December 31, 2002. Funding requirements for defined benefit plans are determined by government regulations, not SFAS 87. We anticipate that we will make a cash contribution to our plans of $141 million in 2003.

The calculation of pension expense and our pension liability requires the use of a number of assumptions. Changes in these assumptions can result in different expense and liability amounts, and future actual experience can differ from the assumptions. We believe that the two most critical assumptions are the expected long-term rate of return on plan assets and the assumed discount rate.

We assumed that our plans' assets would generate a long-term rate of return of 9.0% at December 31, 2002. This rate is lower than the assumed rate of 9.5% used at both December 31, 2001 and 2000. We develop our expected long-term rate of return assumption by evaluating input from the trustee managing the plans' assets, including the trustee's review of asset class return expectations by several consultants and economists as well as long-term inflation assumptions.

2003 that it actually planned to use a 9 percent return for 2003 and projected its pension expenses would climb by $1.9 billion, or about $2.55 a share, resulting in earnings of $4.75 for 2003, about 25 percent lower than 2002 earnings.) Dropping the interest rate down to 6.5 percent, as Buffett suggested, would cause pension expenses to climb to $7.83 a share, which, based on First Call estimates, would turn GM's profit into a loss.

During that same January conference call, GM announced that the company's pension obligations exceeded its pension assets by $19.3 billion in 2002, more than twice the size of the $9.1 billion gap in 2001. Executives also noted that shareholder equity would decline sharply because of GM's pension woes. GM executives spent nearly two hours of that telephone call explaining to analysts and money managers what it was doing to shore up its pension plan. GM's CFO, John Devine, told analysts that there was a "substantial pension drag on both earnings and cash flow."

"This is the No. 1 topic with institutional investors," says Zion. "They all want to know how the balance sheet is going to be impacted and when they will see earnings decline because of pensions."

Pensions don't always warrant this much attention. Remember, there are plenty of companies—about 140 in the S&P 500—that don't offer pensions, so if you only invest in those companies, figuring out Pension-land isn't worth your time.

And, perhaps most important, pensions really become a problem only when the market declines for several years in a row. During the boom times in the 1990s, few people were worrying about the impact that all that extra pension income was having on earnings.

Says Halford: "It's one of those things that when everything is going well, it's not a factor. But when you have three years of a downturn, it becomes a very big problem."

CHAPTER 8

Debt by Many Other Names

BY THE SPRING of 2002, when Yahoo! sent out its annual report to shareholders, the tech wreck was already two years old and had claimed over 500 Internet companies, including such popular stocks as Etoys.com, Excite@Home, and Pets.com. So it was certainly understandable that Yahoo! would want to tout its ability to survive in such a punishing market.

Five separate times in its 2001 annual report, Yahoo! noted its strong balance sheet and the $1.5 billion in cash and marketable securities it had on hand. In his letter to shareholders, Yahoo! Chairman and Chief Executive Officer (CEO) Terry Semel even bragged that the company had "no debt"—another big positive that set Yahoo! apart from many of the Internet companies that had already failed and those that were still struggling to survive.[1]

And indeed there was no debt on Yahoo!'s balance sheet, at least as far as accounting rules were concerned. But the company did provide a helpful hint to investors in its "Committments and

Contingencies" footnote that it had some sizable debt-like obligations—items that credit rating agencies like Standard and Poor's (S&P) and Moody's treat as if they were liabilities. On its balance sheet, Yahoo! provided a hint to investors on how they should consider this footnote. In the liabilities section, where debt is normally listed, Yahoo! included a blank line called "Commitments and Contingencies" directing investors to footnote 11.[2] Investors who picked up on that clue would have seen that Yahoo! was on the hook for more than $300 million to cover various operating leases and other real estate obligations for its new headquarters in Sunnyvale, California.

Yahoo! was hardly the only company to push real estate obligations off of its balance sheet, although the company's claim of no debt, while technically accurate, certainly seemed a bit brazen in the post-Enron world. Hundreds, if not thousands, of publicly traded companies structured similar real estate transactions and crafted other types of corporate arrangements whose primary purpose was to keep debt and assets off of their balance sheets.

"The perception was that if the accounting rules allowed it and if it reflected positively on earnings, why wouldn't you do it? Companies were just playing by the rules," says one New York–based real estate executive whose company set up hundreds of deals worth billions of dollars, many of them structured in such a way as to be kept off of the balance sheets of publicly traded companies.

The very nature of off-balance sheet obligations can make it difficult for investors, particularly individual investors, to begin to understand the size and scope of the problem. Accounting analyst Jack Ciesielski, a frequent critic of the way companies manipulate existing accounting rules, notes that many of these deals were designed deliberately so that public companies would not have to reveal things they'd rather keep secret.

Enron, of course, was the most famous example of how off-balance sheet obligations can really wreak havoc. A 2,000-page report released in March 2003 by a U.S. bankruptcy court examiner found that the company had created hundreds of off-balance sheet transactions, enabling it to underestimate its debt massively. In 2000, the last year that Enron filed an annual report with the Securities and Exchange Commission (SEC), the company reported $10.2 billion in short- and long-term debt, when in reality the company's debt was more than twice that—$22.1 billion, according to the bankruptcy court report.[3] Many of its off-balance sheet arrangements, called special purpose entities (SPEs) in accounting-speak (or sinful parent enterprises, as Ciesielski calls them in his newsletter, *The Analyst's Accounting Observer*), were tied to the company's ability to maintain a certain stock price and, in some cases, debt ratings. When the stock started falling in the summer of 2001, Enron had to come up with additional collateral that it did not have, sending the company into a death spiral.

Until accounting rules on off-balance sheet obligations changed in January 2003, largely due to Enron's massive abuses, companies were not required to provide much information to investors on their off-balance sheet activities. Those that did might have included a few cryptically worded sentences buried deep in the company's footnote on Commitments and Contingencies.

"It was very difficult to get any information on this," says Dave Halford, an equity portfolio manager for Madison Investment Advisors and the Mosaic Fund Group, a highly respected fund. "And there was not a lot of difference between what Enron was doing and what other companies were doing." As a result, Halford

What Is a Special Purpose Entity?

An SPE is a separate corporate structure financed through debt taken on by a particular company, but designed to keep both assets and liabilities off of that company's balance sheet. Companies, typically working with banks or other financial services firms, form SPEs to finance various expenses, including real estate, research and development, and fleets of cars or airplanes. The lender provides the financing and invests 3 percent of its own money or finds someone else to come up with the 3 percent (the minimum required to permit the SPE to remain off the parent company's books). The remaining 97 percent is financed and becomes an obligation for the company —albeit one that remains off its balance sheet. New rules issued by the Financial Accounting Standards Board (FASB) in January 2003 bump up the minimum investment requirement to 10 percent and require companies to place most SPEs back on their balance sheets, making them much less attractive.

says, he tended to avoid companies that he believed had big off-balance sheet exposure or that perhaps hinted at it in their footnotes, even if he wasn't entirely sure of the size of the obligation.

The new rules, however, make it far easier for professionals like Halford as well as individual investors to get a much clearer picture of off-balance sheet activity. In their 2002 10-Ks, many companies started to provide a virtual treasure-trove of information on their off-balance sheet activity, though much of it was still written in accounting-speak. Simply because so much of this information was hidden from investors in the past makes this all the more important for investors to pay attention to.

"Most of what the disclosures will be talking about will be things that investors will see pretty clearly for the first time," says Jim Mountain, a partner at accounting firm Deloitte & Touche. "You can't speculate, but investors may hear some fairly dramatic numbers in narrow, isolated circumstances."[4]

Why should individual investors care about off-balance sheet obligations? Because they can mask a company's true financial condition, making it look stronger than it really is. Pushing debt and other obligations off the balance sheet changes many of the numbers that investors typically use to evaluate a particular

SEARCH TIP

Even with the new rules, finding things that have been pushed off the balance sheet can be tricky because different companies use different words to describe their off-balance sheet transactions. After downloading a 10-K or 10-Q, try using search words such as "off-balance sheet," "Commitments and Contingencies," "operating lease," or "Special Purpose Entity." Words relating to the new rules include "Variable Interest Entity" (VIE) or "FIN 46," the formal name for the new FASB rule. Securitizations, where a company sells off its accounts payable or other receivables, are another large form of off-balance sheet activity. You're likely to find information on all of these in both the Management's Discussion and Analysis (MD&A) section and in the footnotes, though it will rarely be concentrated in one place.

To appreciate how much things have changed in the post-Enron world, compare a 10-K for 2002, the first year that some companies really began providing details on their off-balance sheet obligations, to one from 2000. It will be relatively easy to spot some big changes at many companies.

company, including net income, cash flow, and of course, the company's level of debt.

Most individual investors, when they consider debt at all, typically look at the short- and long-term debt listed on the balance sheet. But given the size and popularity of off-balance sheet transactions during the 1990s—some estimates put the number at trillions of dollars in these liabilities sitting in the accounting netherworld—just looking at the debt listed on a company's balance sheet meant that investors were barely scratching the surface. One simple way for individual investors to think about off-balance sheet transactions— which often involve real estate transactions—is to imagine how your bank account balance would improve if only you didn't have to account for the monthly mortgage payment.

In 2002, as outrage over Enron's off-balance sheet deals spread from Congress to the SEC to FASB, new laws were passed and new rules issued that were designed to restrict the use of such artificial balance sheet sweeteners. Congress weighed in by passing the Sarbanes-Oxley Act in July 2002, and FASB and the SEC each issued rules designed to deal with off-balance sheet transactions in January 2003. For companies that are on a calendar year, the new rules take effect in the fall of 2003.

In its new rule, known as FIN 46, FASB even coined a new name, variable interest entity, which broadened the definition of off-balance sheet transactions, making it harder—at least in theory— for companies to continue keeping these deals off of their balance sheets. The new rules also require that any company that has the majority of risks and rewards from the off-balance sheet activity move it back onto their balance sheet, says Ronald Lott, the FASB project manager who helped to develop the new rules.

The SEC's new rules focus primarily on how companies should disclose off-balance sheet transactions to investors. Companies now are required to provide details in both written and chart form about their off-balance sheet transactions in a separate section of their MD&A every quarter. (In the past, companies typically only provided limited disclosure in their 10-K filings.) While the rules don't prohibit companies from creating off-balance sheet arrangements, they create a higher hurdle for companies looking to keep such transactions off their balance sheets.[*]

"There are good reasons to have separate entities," says Lott. "But I really can't see a good reason for a company to leave it off of their books."

Of course, Lott and others note that companies may be able to find a way around the new rules; noting that it's certainly happened in the past. Although many companies disclosed numerous off-balance sheet transactions for the first time in their 2002 10-Ks, many other companies simply stated that they were still evaluating the new FASB and SEC rules. At those companies, it was likely that the CFO and outside accountants were working overtime to make sure that these off-balance sheet obligations never saw the light of day by the time the new rules went into effect.

---

[*] However, the new SEC rules on off-balance sheet disclosure were watered down after intense lobbying from accounting and business groups and despite specific language passed by Congress in the Sarbanes-Oxley Act. An earlier draft of the SEC rules on off-balance sheet transactions would have required companies to include obligations that had a "remote" possibility of having a material impact on the company. But in its final rules, the SEC decided to adopt the much more narrowly worded "reasonably likely" language. In their comment letters to the SEC, many accounting and business groups said that using the word remote would require companies to disclose too many off-balance sheet obligations, which they said would only be "confusing to investors," a specious argument if ever there was one. That subtle difference in wording could be enough to keep many companies from disclosing some off-balance sheet transactions to investors.

RED FLAG

Be wary of any company that says it's still evaluating the situation. Companies know full well what's being kept off of their balance sheets. The only thing they're evaluating are ways to continue keeping it out of sight.

Says Lott: "I hesitate to predict what might happen because I know there are people working hard to get around this."

Still, if even some of what has typically been pushed off balance sheet makes it into the financial statements, the impact has the potential to be huge. By some estimates, public companies have over $1 trillion worth of net-lease arrangements—a popular technique used to finance office buildings and factories that enables a company to keep debt and assets off of its balance sheet. Another $700 billion in asset-backed commercial paper arrangements have also largely been kept off balance sheet. In addition, over $100 billion of synthetic leases are estimated to be off balance sheet. Still, because nobody really knows the extent of off-balance sheet arrangements, many of these numbers are just a guess.

In its 2002 10-K filing, for example, McDonald's Corp. provided details on an off-balance sheet arrangement that it had with a company called System Capital Corp. (SCC), which provides funding and supplies, including real estate financing to McDonald's Corp. and its franchisees. Although the company had provided a few preliminary details about SCC for the first time in its 2001 filing with the SEC, the 2002 10-K provided much greater details on a web of interrelated companies. The filing noted that SCC, which is partially owned by McDonald's and six other partners, had made $900 million in loans to McDonald's franchisees, had leased $500

What Is a Synthetic Lease?

A synthetic lease is a type of arrangement that permits a company to enjoy the benefits of property ownership, primarily tax deductions, by indirectly financing the property through an SPE. Doing this reduces debt and keeps the obligation off a company's balance sheet. In a typical synthetic lease, a company's financial partner—a bank or other financial institution—creates an SPE to own a piece of property, say a new headquarters building for a company. The company is required to make annual lease payments for the term of the lease, typically five to seven years, and then has the ability to purchase the property, refinance, or sign another short-term lease. Rent payments typically are significantly lower than in a traditional lease because the company is still on the hook for a large, balloon-like payment at the end of the lease. Many synthetic leases also provide a guarantee that the company will purchase the property for a certain amount, leading to problems if either the real estate market or the company's own fortunes decline sharply, something that happened at many companies in Silicon Valley. These leases were very popular in the 1990s but became highly controversial in the wake of the Enron meltdown. In March 2002, Krispy Kreme disclosed plans to use a synthetic lease to build a new $130 million doughnut factory. But it quickly canceled its plans after several journalists reported on the company's plans.

million of land to McDonald's Corp., and had loaned $300 million to McDonald's suppliers. McDonald's also noted that an SCC subsidiary, Golden Funding Corp. (a word play on McDonald's Golden Arches) had $1.7 billion in commercial paper and medium-term loans as of December 31, 2002. McDonald's disclosure did not say whether it had guaranteed any part of Golden Funding's debt, although presumably, as a partial owner of SCC, it would have some obligation.

Still, McDonald's disclosure on its off-balance sheet obligations pales in comparison to those made in 2002 by large banks, insurance companies, and other financial services firms, which traditionally have been among the biggest players in off-balance sheet financing. That's because many of these companies were heavily involved in setting up and financing many of the off-balance sheet arrangements at other companies. In its 2002 10-K filing, Citigroup Inc. disclosed $236.4 billion in potential exposure from off-balance sheet arrangements, compared with the $58.6 billion it disclosed in its 2001 filing.[5] And this was even before the company was required to provide significant details on its off-balance sheet arrangements.

"Companies are going to have to hang out their dirty linen and start disclosing all of their off-balance sheet arrangements," says the New York real estate professional. "The companies that are strong financially are going to look at this and yawn. But it's a different story for those companies that are weaker. They don't want to put this on their balance sheets."

Although many professional investors and the debt rating agencies note that they've been adjusting their numbers to reflect off-balance sheet transactions for years, not all of the deals were clearly visible, even to those who knew where to look. Some companies—like Yahoo!—included a line on their balance sheets directing investors to the Commitments and Contingencies footnote. But others, including AOL Time Warner, provided limited details, even in their footnotes.

Because disclosure requirements weren't as stringent before 2003, rating agencies and some professional investors typically asked different companies about their off-balance sheet transactions and hoped that the companies were being truthful. Representatives of S&P, for example, testified before Congress in March 2002 that they had asked Enron about its off-balance sheet transactions, and said that the company failed to provide S&P with the full picture. An S&P spokeswoman says that Enron's failure to come clean is the primary reason that the rating agency failed to downgrade Enron's debt until just before the company filed for bankruptcy.

Individual investors, however, didn't have that same opportunity. Indeed, before Enron, the overwhelming majority of individual investors probably didn't even know that there was such a thing as an off-balance sheet transaction. Companies certainly didn't tout the fact that they had off-balance sheet obligations. Nor could investors have imagined that something that they didn't even know existed could have such serious consequences for the companies they owned stock in.

Real estate wasn't the only thing that moved off of the balance sheet during the dot-com boom. Banks and financial services companies were able to generate large fees by using the existing accounting rules to move all sorts of big-ticket expenses into the accounting netherworld, including research and development expenses, large equipment purchases, and other types of purchases that were financed with off-balance sheet debt. GE Capital's Corporate Aircraft Group, for example, touted off-balance sheet financing for corporate jets as a way to "receive ownership tax benefits without incurring the debt."[6]

"Some of this stuff is just common sense, " says former SEC chief accountant Lynn Turner. "If you have a lot of debt, leasings, and spread, how could it be off the balance sheet?"

For years, synthetic leases seemed almost too good to be true because they provided companies with the tax benefits of owning property without having to put the debt on the balance sheet. During the boom, companies eager to put their best foot forward couldn't seem to get enough of these leases. But in August 2002, Inktomi, a once-popular Internet software maker whose shares had traded as high as $241 during the Internet bubble, experienced firsthand how synthetic leases can lead to big problems when the real estate market is declining and the demand for its products drops off significantly.

Two years earlier, near the height of its popularity, Inktomi had entered into a synthetic lease to cover the cost of building a 261,000-square-foot corporate campus in Foster City, California. Working through an SPE created by Deutsche Bank, Inktomi financed the purchase through debt and signed an operating lease that saved the company millions in rent and kept the obligation off of its balance sheet. But in June 2002, with Inktomi deep in red ink, it began to violate the terms of the operating lease. By August Inktomi's lenders said it had to come up with the entire $114 million that it had guaranteed, money that basically tapped out its remaining cash. In December, Inktomi sold the two buildings to a pension plan for about one-third of what it had spent in August. With its cash gone and without a way to raise more money, the company was acquired by Yahoo! in early 2003 for around $235 million.

Would Inktomi have been able to survive had it not taken such a big hit on its real estate? Probably not, given the sluggish demand for its product and the surging popularity of one of its competitors, Google. But chances are that Inktomi would have been able to find a better use for its remaining cash than buying and quickly selling for a huge loss two buildings it no longer needed.

Just because there's more information available on off-balance sheet obligations, doesn't mean that investors should ignore plain old vanilla debt, the type that is more familiar to investors and has always been disclosed in the footnotes. It's important to look at both short- and long-term debt and note which direction the numbers are moving in. Debt isn't necessarily a bad thing, particularly for companies in capital-intensive businesses. And when interest rates are declining, as they have been since 2000, debt actually can be a practical way to grow a business.

Yet too much debt can lead to serious problems, particularly when the on-balance sheet debt represents only part of the company's total obligations. There are different schools of thought on how to determine whether a company has taken on too much debt. Some industries are simply prone to more debt than others, making it hard to come up with a catchall standard. That's one of the reasons why it makes sense to compare two different companies in the same industry.

Some professionals like to look at a company's debt to equity ratio, which is total debt divided by shareholder equity. Others look at long-term debt to total capital (equity plus all debt) or the interest coverage ratio (pretax income plus interest expense divided by interest expense). Still, these ratios can be very misleading. For example, at Lucent Technologies, the debt to total capital ratio

SEARCH TIP

Most companies devote a separate footnote just to their debt. Look closely at the mix between long-term and short-term debt, and also look for when that debt is coming due.

137

declined between 1998 and 1999 to 37.6 percent from 34.1 percent, which was clearly a positive, even though the company's short- and long-term debt rose by over 50 percent that year.[7] How was Lucent able to lower its debt to total capital ratio? By increasing shareholder equity, a number that Jeff Middleswart of the accounting newsletter *Behind the Numbers* says is one of the easiest numbers to manipulate on the balance sheet.

"You can see many companies tout their debt to equity declining, but all they are doing is taking actions to increase the equity balance, which lowers the ratio," says Middleswart.

In his book *Take on the Street,* former SEC Chairman Arthur Levitt suggests a very simple way to look at debt by looking at the balance sheet and comparing cash to total debt. A big gap, as there was at Enron at the end of 2000, should be a warning sign, Levitt wrote.[8]

It's always a good idea to at least skim a company's debt footnote, something many professional investors are paying more attention to these days. This footnote provides a debt breakdown, including the split between long- and short-term debt, the average interest rate, any requirements the company must meet in order to prevent defaulting on the debt, and who gets paid first if a default occurs. (Hint: It's never the shareholder.)

Even without getting bogged down in the details, often it's relatively easy to spot a potential problem. For example, investors who did a quick skim of Lucent Technologies' debt footnote in its 1999 10-K would have seen that the interest rate on the company's long-term debt and secured borrowings had climbed to 9.7 percent from 7.9 percent a year earlier even though rates were generally falling.[9] Investors who picked up on that shift might have realized that things weren't as rosy as they appeared to be at Lucent.

CHAPTER 9

Five Common
Ingredients

A NYONE WHO'S EVER been to a chili cookoff knows that each of the different teams uses its own special ingredients to achieve its own unique flavor. Some might add beer, or chocolate, or some other secret ingredient. But the basic components—meat, onions, tomatoes, peppers and chili powder—tend to remain the same from pot to pot.

Analyzing the fine print in a 10-K or 10-Q has more than a few things in common with a big pot of chili. At some companies, one or two "ingredients" stand out and warrant extra attention by the judges, or investors. After all, not every company offers pensions or has a lot of off-balance sheet obligations, so it makes little sense to spend time trying to analyze those ingredients. But a few common footnotes remain important no matter who's standing over the pot.

No list, of course, can ever be exhaustive. But money managers and others who spend their time reading the footnotes say that their analysis would be incomplete without looking at these five footnotes:

1. Taxes

2. Derivatives

3. "The Others"

4. Legal issues

5. Segment breakdown

TAXES

Before analyzing the debt, poking around through the pension footnote, or even reviewing the receivables, Robert Olstein, who manages about $2.1 billion, heads straight for the tax footnote. The footnote, which Olstein says few people bother with, can tell him almost instantly whether a company is using accounting smoke and mirrors to make its results look better than they really are.

"Over the years, this [footnote] has consistently been one of my most reliable indicators," says Olstein. "It lets me know how realistic their financial statements are and whether they're in accordance with economic reality."

One of those little-known secrets when it comes to corporate financials is that companies report two sets of results: one to their shareholders and another set to the Internal Revenue Service (IRS). While the two numbers are rarely even close to one another, both can be calculated in strict accordance with respective IRS and generally accepted accounting principles (GAAP) rules. In general, the earnings that are reported to investors are almost always higher than those reported to the IRS for pretty obvious reasons: to make the company look better for investors and worse for the IRS. One

IRS study found that the gap between the two numbers began growing sharply in the 1990s—a good indication that many companies were using tax techniques to squeeze out extra earnings.[1]

Companies report their taxes on the income statement, in a line that's usually labeled "Income Tax Provision." But that's not the amount of money that the company sends to the IRS. Finding that number requires flipping to the tax footnote and looking for the company's disclosure on its current taxes. The difference between what the company is supposed to pay and what it actually does pay is called the "Net Deferred Tax Asset (or Liability)." In the tax footnote, companies typically provide three years' worth of information on their tax situation, and it's important to pay attention to which way the numbers are going.

It's pretty easy to get lost in this footnote, which is often heavy on numbers and short on text. Many companies, in fact, simply present a series of charts, leaving it up to investors to figure things out. Ted Oglove, who first started looking at tax footnotes back in the 1960s and has studied thousands of them, says that over the years, this footnote has become increasingly complicated, making it hard even for many pros to understand.

"We know that companies report a lot less income to the IRS, but that number is very hard to find," says Oglove, noting that

SEARCH TIP

Head to the tax footnote to spot any differences between the results that companies report to shareholders and the results reported to the IRS. While some discrepancies are normal, due to two sets of rules, large differences should be carefully explained and examined.

few investors have access to a company's corporate tax returns. "Yet the bigger the gap between the two numbers, the bigger the problem."

When Olstein reads the tax footnote, he's looking for how good a job the company does in explaining away the difference between the income it reports to shareholders and the income it reports to the IRS. In 1998, after reading Sunbeam's 1997 10-K, for example, Olstein noticed that there was a sizable gap—about $76 million—between the earnings Sunbeam was reporting to shareholders and the earnings it was reporting to the IRS. This difference raised questions for him over whether the company was manipulating its numbers. As it turns out, the questionable tax accounting was just the tip of the iceberg at Sunbeam. The company wound up filing for bankruptcy and restating six quarters of results and was charged by the Securities and Exchange Commission (SEC) with large-scale accounting fraud.

At Enron, a massive congressional investigation found that the company had created a tax department "with the primary purpose of manufacturing financial statement income."[2] The investigation found that Enron paid no federal income taxes between 1996 and 1999, despite reporting large profits to shareholders during those years. Some of this information would have been clear to investors who had read Enron's tax footnote. In 1999, the same year that the company reported $1.1 billion in income, the company listed its current taxes at $83 million, a fraction of what it should have paid, although, as the investigation revealed, it didn't even pay that amount.[3]

One of the quick things investors can focus on in this footnote is the company's effective tax rate (ETR). Even though, theoretically, the corporate tax rate is 35 percent, few companies actually pay that amount. For example, General Electric's (GE) tax rate in 2002 was 19.9 percent, compared with 28.3 percent in 2001.[4]

Although approximately 60 percent of all companies in the Standard and Poor's (S&P) 500 pay taxes in the range of 30 to 40 percent, investors really want to hone in on those companies that fall outside of this range, according to a study by asset management firm New Amsterdam Partners. The study found that between 1998 and 2000, companies whose tax rates were outside the normal range made for significantly worse investments. In particular, companies whose tax rates were lower than 30 percent performed particularly poorly when compared with companies that fell in the 30 to 40 percent range and even those whose tax rates were above 40 percent.[5]

RED FLAG

Tax rates that fall outside the normal range of 30 to 40 percent often can be a sign of tax tinkering at the company. Any negative tax rate is a particular cause for concern, especially if the company is reporting a profit to shareholders.

The other important thing to focus on in the tax footnote is the trend for both deferred tax assets and liabilities. This is where the company explains how its tax numbers differ from its shareholder numbers. All you really need to look for here are any large swings.

More than a year before it filed for bankruptcy, Global Crossing reported sharp spikes in both its deferred tax liabilities —$479.3 million in 1999 compared with $10.2 million in 1998— and its deferred tax assets—$61.5 million in 1999 compared with $500,000 the year before. In addition, the company reported a tax rate of 107.8 percent in 1999, even though it was incorporated in

Bermuda, a well-known tax haven, notes Michelle Clayman, chief investment officer for New Amsterdam Partners, which manages $1.4 billion. Indeed, the strange tax rate alone should have been enough for investors to realize that something highly unusual was going on at the company, particularly given that the company was incorporated in Bermuda. Global Crossing disclosed this in the company's tax footnote.

"It made the financial reporting books look a lot better than they really were, but it was misleading to shareholders," says Clayman. "All of this was there for investors to see, but people got swept up in the bubble."

DERIVATIVES

Unless you're a glutton for punishment or have an unusually bad case of insomnia, you probably don't want to devote too much of your time trying to figure out derivatives. First of all, even if you had the time, most companies don't provide anywhere near enough information on their derivatives contracts for investors to figure out what's truly going on. It's kind of like trying to solve a jigsaw puzzle that's missing more than half the pieces.

Second, given the wide variation in derivatives contracts, which can be set up for just about anything, whole books can be written on trying to interpret these exceedingly complicated transactions. A relatively straightforward definition, courtesy of Citigroup's 10-K, defines derivatives as "a contract or agreement whose value is derived from changes in interest rates, foreign exchange rates, prices of securities or commodities or financial or commodity indices."[6]

Few people—including many pros—seem to understand how derivatives really work. Even Warren Buffett, in his 2002 letter to shareholders, said that he and Berkshire Hathaway Vice Chairman Charlie Munger—two incredibly experienced and sophisticated investors—often found it difficult to gauge a company's true exposure to risk after reading that company's derivatives footnote.

"We view them [derivatives] as time bombs, both for the parties that deal in them and the economic system," Buffett said in his annual letter, which devoted three pages and some unusually strong language to the damage he believes derivatives are causing to world financial markets. "Derivatives are financial weapons of mass destruction, carrying dangers that, while now latent, are potentially lethal."[7]

RED FLAG

Given the size of the derivatives market, many companies use them heavily. Be wary of companies that provide limited disclosure here. Even if you don't understand every word—and most of us won't—you probably want to avoid companies that seem unusually close-mouthed when it comes to derivatives.

Buffett knows firsthand the dangers of derivatives. General Re Securities, a derivatives business that Berkshire Hathaway acquired in 1998 when it purchased reinsurance firm General Re, lost $173 million in 2002, one of the few negatives at Berkshire that year. In his letter to shareholders, Buffett noted that Berkshire Hathaway was working hard to get out of the derivatives business, but found that winding down derivatives contracts, some of which stretch on for 20 years or more, was incredibly difficult.[8]

Yet thousands of companies rely heavily on derivatives to generate paper profits and losses that can help enhance earnings. According to the Derivatives Study Center, the derivatives market was worth over $127 trillion at the end of 2002, up from $3 trillion in 1990. At banks and other financial services companies, the derivatives footnote is particularly important to pay attention to. JP Morgan Chase, the world's largest derivatives trader, has over $27 trillion worth of contracts on its books.[9] Citigroup is another huge player. In its 2002 10-K filing, the word "derivative" was used more than 100 times, making it hard for all but the most passive Citigroup investors to ignore.

Derivatives sometimes are listed on the income statement and the balance sheet as a separate line, though they're usually lumped into the "other" category. Even so, very little of the risk is visible to investors, notes Lynn Turner, the former chief accountant for the SEC.

In an attempt to help investors understand, some companies are beginning to provide more information on their derivatives contracts. For example, GE devoted more than three pages of footnotes to what it describes as "financial instruments" in its 10-K. IBM also improved its disclosure in its 2002 10-K. But most companies still provide as little information as possible on derivatives.

Perhaps the best approach when it comes to understanding derivatives is to do what Olstein does: "I just go with my gut. If I can't understand it or don't trust what they're doing, I just keep away."

"THE OTHERS"

While it may be tempting to overlook "The Others"—Other Income, Other Expenses, Other Assets, and Other Liabilities—thinking that anything that's labeled this obtusely couldn't possibly be all that important, these catchall categories can often provide important clues about a company.

That's because at many companies, it's much more common to see big swings in numbers that have the word "other" in their names than in just about any other place on the income statement or balance sheet, except for perhaps postmerger numbers. For example, IBM reported $227 million in "other expenses" at the end of 2002, compared with $353 million in "other income" in 2001 and $990 million in "other income" in 2000, a $1.2 billion difference over two years.[10] At GE, "other assets" of $93.2 billion for 2002 were up nearly 22 percent over 2001's $76.6 billion and represented over 16 percent of the company's total assets listed on its balance sheet in 2002.[11] Even at large companies like GE and IBM, these shifts are simply too big for most investors to ignore.

What sorts of things get dumped into "the others"? The creativity here is limited only by the skills of the chief financial officer and the company's outside accountants. The ingredients that go into this accounting stew can change from quarter to quarter and

 **SEARCH TIP**

Take a quick look at both the income statement and the balance sheet to see whether there have been any big changes over the past year in the oft-overlooked "others."

year to year. Typically they include everything from plain-vanilla interest income to complicated hedging techniques, such as derivatives.

Companies often provide a few basic details about what goes into the recipe in the Management's Discussion and Analysis (MD&A) section. In its MD&A, IBM said that the primary reason for the spike in "other expense" in 2002 was $513 million spent in the second and fourth quarters of the year on something simply referred to as "the actions taken by the company."[12] But the real meat of what goes into this number is often found in the footnotes.

Some companies make you dig for the information. In IBM's case, the company sprinkled the information on "other income" across four different footnotes in its 2002 10-K, including a footnote within the footnotes that the bulk of its "other expense" came from losing $223 million on the sale of a microchip plant near Binghamton, New York.[13]

RED FLAG

Be wary any time a company makes you work overtime to find out what's being included in other income/expenses or other assets/liabilities.

Because so many investors tend to overlook "the others" and because it is so easy to hide things there, many research-driven pros like to poke around through these numbers. Some, including Olstein, even use this as a gauge to see how open the company is being when it comes to its disclosures.

Many companies, including IBM, have improved their disclosure on "other" items substantially. Just two years earlier, in its 2000 10-K, IBM provided only one line about its other income of $617 million, noting in its MD&A that it had increased 10.9 percent that year—a simple fact that anyone looking at the income statement could have easily calculated.[14]

LEGAL ISSUES

Companies get sued all the time—by customers, by contractors, by employees and/or investors, and even sometimes by various branches of government. The overwhelming majority of these lawsuits are not worth paying much attention to. Even if the company eventually loses or settles, its costs usually are insignificant (or "not material" to use the same lingo that many companies do), at least as far as most investors are concerned.

So why pay any attention to this footnote at all? Because all it takes is one large verdict to send a stock into virtual free fall.

Over the past few years, in part prompted by the post-Enron *glasnost*, companies have begun providing many more details on pending lawsuits and other legal actions that they are facing,

SEARCH TIP

Don't expect to find a smoking gun in this footnote. Companies often write more about the larger suits, but it's important to take the entire body of lawsuits into account. Sometimes a suit that garners little notice can turn into a big problem.

including many suits that would never have been considered material before. The problem with these long lists of lawsuits, of course, is that it becomes all but impossible for most of us to figure out which suits are truly important.

For example, Altria Corp., previously known as Phillip Morris, provided over six pages of footnotes on pending litigation in its 2001 annual report, but included only one brief line on a lawsuit filed in Illinois against its Phillip Morris USA unit. The suit claimed that the company had deceived smokers into thinking light cigarettes were safer than regular cigarettes. In its 2001 10-K, lumped together with 11 other suits that the company described as Light/ Ultra Light cases, Altria noted that the Illinois case had been certified as a class action and was heading to trial in August 2002.

In March 2003, after the company lost the $10.1 billion case, an Illinois Circuit Court Judge ordered Phillip Morris USA to post a $12 billion bond in order to appeal the ruling. Posting a bond of that size—even for a company as large as Phillip Morris—was impossible, company executives said, prompting both the company and Wall Street to talk about the possibility of bankruptcy.[15] Although the bond requirement eventually was reduced to $6 billion, in the weeks after the verdict, Altria's stock fell sharply and its bonds were downgraded by several of the major bond rating agencies, catching many investors by surprise. Also caught unawares were investors in Kraft Foods Inc.; even though its stock and bonds trade separately, Kraft is controlled by Altria. Kraft's shareholders, however, didn't even receive the one-line warning about the Illinois lawsuit in their annual report.

SEGMENT BREAKDOWN

Although the segment breakdown footnote, which often appears at the end of the 10-K or 10-Q, may seem like a bit of an afterthought, many professional investors believe it's a mistake to treat it as such. Indeed, Dick Weiss, co-manager of the $2.5 billion Strong Opportunity Fund, says the segment breakdown is something he reviews closely. "I try to find the mathematical relationships to see if things are really what the company is saying," Weiss says.

Under GAAP, companies are required to provide segment breakdowns of their major business units as well as geographical breakdowns and a brief description of their major customers. The more information, Weiss says, the better because it allows him to get a more complete picture of the company's strengths and weaknesses without having to rely on the company's spin. Many companies, in an effort to provide greater transparency on their financials, are providing much more detail than they ever did before by expanding the number of reporting units.

Boeing Corp., for example, has expanded its reporting units several times since 2001 and began providing data on seven different business segments in the first quarter of 2003, more than twice the number it was reporting just two years earlier.[16] Sun Microsystems, however, has taken the opposite tack, going from three reporting segments in 1999 down to two segments by the fall of 2002.[17]

RED FLAG

Be wary of companies that shrink the number of business segments they report to investors for no apparent reason.

What specific things does Weiss advise investors to look for here? Pretty much anything that sticks out. If one segment seems to be generating the bulk of operating income or accounts for the bulk of assets, or if most of its revenues are generated from a particular region of the world, it may make sense to pay closer attention. The number and types of calculations that can be done with these breakdowns are limited only by the amount of time you're willing to put in.

For example, skimming the 2002 segment breakdown for Caterpillar Corp. shows that a growing portion of the heavy equipment manufacturer's assets are in its Finance and Insurance Services division, even though that segment accounts for less than 10 percent of sales and less than 20 percent of profits.[18] Because the bulk of those assets are primarily loans to customers and dealers, any spike in the number of bad loans—something highly likely in a prolonged bad economy—would have a big impact on Caterpillar's bottom line.

Says Weiss: "There's all sorts of things that are in this footnote that aren't in the [earnings] press release or that analysts don't pick up on."

CHAPTER 10

Changing
the World

ICTURE THIS: It's high noon in New York's Central Park. An unassuming middle-age man from Colorado—the type of person who might easily be mistaken for a tourist—takes out some rope and starts to work. Soon dozens of other men—dressed in expensive suits and Hermès ties—are dangling from the park's stately elm and maple trees. CNBC is broadcasting the event live. Millions of investors—people who lost their entire life savings simply because they were too trusting or didn't know any better—watch the scene and start to cheer.

It'll never happen, of course. But Lynn Turner, the former chief accountant for the Securities and Exchange Comminssion (SEC), says this might just be the best way to solve what he delicately describes as the real lack of honesty plaguing corporate America.

"There's still a clear mentality in corporate America that they don't want to make any changes," says Turner, who after leaving the SEC in August 2001 began teaching at Colorado State University's

Center for Quality Financial Reporting. While the Sarbanes-Oxley Act, the supposedly get-tough legislation that was signed into law on July 30, 2002, is better than nothing, Turner doesn't expect it to solve many problems. "If you give me ten feet of rope and a tree, I can fix it so much quicker than Sarbanes-Oxley can."

When Sarbanes-Oxley was signed into law, investors were told that it would essentially eliminate future Enrons and WorldComs by making corporate executives and their boards more accountable for their actions (or inactions). We were led to believe that the certification requirement alone—which requires both the chief executive officer (CEO) and the chief financial officer (CFO) to sign the filing and certify that the company's financial results are accurate—would put an end to the excesses of the 1990s once and for all. We were told that the new Accounting Standards Board (ASB) would ride herd over the accountants who were certifying those results and that the threat of a 25-year prison term and steep financial penalties for securities fraud would be an added stop-gap to keep corporate executives honest.

"This law says to every dishonest corporate leader: You will be exposed and punished. The era of low standards and false profits is over," President George W. Bush said during the signing ceremony in the East Room of the White House. "This law says to shareholders that the financial information you receive from a company will be true and reliable."[1]

But that didn't seem to stop Richard M. Scrushy. Scrushy was the former CEO of HealthSouth, a Birmingham, Alabama–based company that he founded in 1984 and built into the nation's largest operator of outpatient rehabilitation centers. In March 2003, the SEC and the Justice Department charged both Scrushy and the company with inflating earnings by more than $2.5 billion and assets by over $800 million over the course of several years. In a secret tape recording made by one of HealthSouth's former CFOs, Scrushy was heard telling William T. Owens to "fix" the results, despite the fact that he had already signed two certification letters attesting to the veracity of those results.

"We just need to get those numbers where we want them to be," Scrushy said on the tape, which was played during a hearing in U.S. District Court in Birmingham. "I want you to go back over the numbers quarter by quarter."[2]

By April 2003, 11 former HealthSouth executives, including all five of the company's former CFOs, had pled guilty to various charges, including securities fraud and falsifying financial information. The HealthSouth case was believed to be the first in the country with charges stemming from the certification requirement in the Sarbanes-Oxley Act.

Clearly, more are likely, though how many more investors will get burned as a result remains unclear. In the secret tape-recording, Scrushy himself said he was convinced that "there are 8,000 companies out there right now that got [expletive deleted] on their balance sheets."[3] Even if Scrushy is way off on his estimates—say there's fewer than 1,000 or maybe he's way way off and there's fewer than 100—that's still a huge potential problem for anyone who owns stock in those companies.

One month after Sarbanes-Oxley was signed, *CFO* magazine found that 17 percent of the CFOs surveyed said they had been pressured at least once by their company's CEO to misrepresent their financial results. A shocking 11 percent of those surveyed said they had been pressured more than three times.[4] Small wonder then that many investors—both professionals and individuals—not to mention accountants and even corporate executives, believe that the new legislation fails to get to the heart of the problem. In March 2003, PricewaterhouseCoopers found that less than one-third of those CFOs surveyed thought that the new laws would be effective in restoring investors' confidence.[5]

"Sarbanes-Oxley is not touching the problem with a ten-foot pole," says Marty Whitman, co-chief investment officer for the Third Avenue Value Fund. After more than 40 years investing in the markets, Whitman has seen more than his share of up-and-down cycles and various attempts at reform. "It didn't get close to the underlying disease of unfettered management enrichment."

After Scrushy was fired from HealthSouth, two board members who took over day-to-day operations began paring the company of various excesses, including grounding the company's fleet of 12 planes and closing luxury boxes at various sport stadiums around the country.[6] HealthSouth investors probably would have never known about those perks absent the accounting scandal. Then again, there were no rules requiring HealthSouth to give shareholders that information. There still aren't, and for the most part, these sorts of juicy perks come to light only after more serious problems crop up.

But right in the company's 2002 proxy, investors were told about Scrushy's $4 million salary and $6.5 million bonus—a more than six-fold increase from his compensation in 1999.[7] Also clearly disclosed in the proxy were Scrushy's $8.3 million in stock options and even his $25.2 million loan that remained outstanding. Turning to the audit committee—a critical committee comprised of members of HealthSouth's board—investors would have seen that they met only once in 2001.[8] Finally, investors could have seen that HealthSouth had done over $200 million worth of business with two separate companies controlled by HealthSouth executives and directors.[9] Any one of these items should have been enough for HealthSouth's investors—not to mention its accountants and the analysts who followed the company—to question what was going on at the company.

Remember: News of the problems at HealthSouth unfolded nine months after both the CEO and CFO certified that the company's financial results were accurate, as required by the Sarbanes-Oxley Act. It happened even though millions of investors had already begun to express their collective disgust with the widespread accounting scandals by cashing out of the market and sitting on the sidelines.

Even after Enron imploded in December 2001, it remained business as usual at many public companies. A survey completed in early 2003 by the SEC of the 10-Ks filed by Fortune 500 companies in 2002 found that many companies were still providing information that was as vague as possible to investors, while still managing to meet the minimum requirements on disclosure since no violations were cited. The SEC's Corporation Finance staff suggested various ways for more than two-thirds of the Fortune 500 companies to improve the information they provided to investors.[10] Still, if the SEC really had wanted to address this problem, it could have provided investors with a list of specific concerns at particular companies, instead of merely noting overall trends. Of course, getting that specific might be a bit too similar to Turner's Central Park solution of a public hanging. Instead, as investors, we are left to figure things out for ourselves.

This is not to imply that all companies are bad or that there haven't been any improvements. For every Enron and WorldCom and Tyco and HealthSouth, there are hundreds, even thousands, of companies whose corporate executives really try to do the right thing for both their companies and their shareholders.

One piece of evidence can be seen by the growth spurt in the size of 10-Ks and 10-Qs in recent years, with many companies providing much more detailed information than ever before to investors, even if the language still is a bit confusing. "It used to be that a Q didn't give you much of anything, but that's really changed," says Dick Weiss, who co-manages the $2.5 billion Strong Opportunity mutual fund. Issues that pre-Enron might have been written off as immaterial, including all sorts of related party transactions, are being talked about openly in SEC filings, notes Brace Brooks, an analyst at fund giant T. Rowe Price.

Some of this new disclosure has been voluntary and some of it has been mandated by the new rules that were developed by both the SEC and the Financial Accounting Standards Board (FASB). As a result of rules that were directly linked to the abuses at Enron, companies are now required to provide details on their off-balance sheet arrangements. Some companies even began moving these special purpose entities or variable interest entities back onto their balance sheets even before they were required to do so. In another effort to improve transparency, many companies began providing side-by-side comparisons of their pro forma and generally accepted accounting principles (GAAP) results before they were required to do so by the SEC in March 2003.

There even has been improvement on expensing options, with a number of large companies voluntarily agreeing to treat the costs as expenses, even though the issue continues to invoke white-hot passions among otherwise rational people. Whether FASB will be able to mandate that companies start expensing options as it tried to back in 1993 remains uncertain, but even if that proposal dies under political pressure, once again at least many more investors are aware of this issue.

There is also renewed hope for investors in the way some companies are handling annual shareholder proposals, something that all too often has not been taken very seriously. Labor unions, large public employee pension funds, religious groups, and individual investors introduced nearly 1,000 shareholder resolutions during the 2002–2003 proxy season, about 20 percent more than in 2002. Such resolutions take aim at a wide variety of issues, from executive compensation to expensing stock options. General Electric alone had 13 shareholder proposals at its 2003 annual meeting. For the most part, these votes are largely ceremonial— SEC rules do not require companies to take any action, even when the proposals attract a majority of the votes—but some companies have begun to pay closer attention to the votes, and some even act on the proposals.

For example, in 2003 Bristol-Myers Squibb did a 180-degree turn when it agreed to allow shareholders to vote annually to elect board members, a proposal it had fought for the past 18-odd years. The proposal was first submitted by shareholder advocate Evelyn Y. Davis in the early 1980s and didn't attract a majority of votes until the company's 2002 annual meeting, when it received 69 percent of the vote. A similar proposal submitted by Davis in 2003 to Dow Jones & Co., which publishes *The Wall Street Journal*, was withdrawn when company executives agreed to make the change before shareholders were set to vote on it.

Small investors like Davis, who have long been derided as gadflys or even kooks—and often were described as such by business journalists—are being taken much more seriously, even by the corporations they're seeking to change. Davis, a septuagenarian who lives in Washington, D.C., and has offered up well over 100 different shareholder proposals over the past 30 years, shifted into high gear in 2003 by introducing resolutions at 28 different companies.

Still, even when investors like Davis win the vote, they often lose. At both Lucent Technologies and Morgan Stanley, shareholders cast a majority of votes in favor of Davis's proposal in 2002 to require annual elections. Neither company decided to move forward on the proposal, however, so Davis decided to submit them again for the 2003 meeting.

Many companies also continue to work hard to keep shareholder proposals off their ballots in the first place to avoid public airing of what they believe are internal matters. During the first six months of its 2003 fiscal year, the SEC received nearly 500 letters from companies looking for permission to exclude shareholder proposals from their proxy statements—more than the SEC had received during all of fiscal 2002. Companies can reject a shareholder proposal as long as the SEC agrees that the proposal involves "ordinary business," a much-abused legal term that companies cite frequently. Reviewing this mountain of requests, noted SEC Commissioner Paul S. Atkins, was taking SEC staffers' time away from reviewing 10-Ks and 10-Qs.

"Stockholders own the corporation and should have the ability to have their opinions aired to their employees in management. That does not seem too much to ask," said Atkins during a speech given at the Council of Institutional Investors' annual meeting in March 2003.[11]

Amen. In Washington and in corporate boardrooms at the nation's approximately 15,000 publicly traded companies, we, the nation's

85 million investors, need to start being taken a lot more seriously than we have been in the past. After all, we own the place.

Even though CEOs and CFOs must now certify their companies' financial results, and even though companies are putting out 10-Qs that are as large as the old 10-Ks and 10-Ks that are as impenetrable as Vergil's *Aeneid*—in Latin—and even though the Accounting Standards Board, after months of delays and false starts, is actually up and running, we, the American investing public, still deserve more.

We need to start raising our voices until we are finally heard. We need to let our elected officials know that individual investors deserve a fair shake too, even if we haven't contributed anything to their reelection campaigns. The stories of people losing their life savings or pensions because of Enron et al. made for great TV and compelling congressional testimony, but much more needs to be done to prevent future accounting fiascoes.

"Shareholders, and especially individual investors, come last. There is no one, in fact, who represents individual investors full time. They are the most overlooked and underrepresented interest group in America," notes former SEC Chairman Arthur Levitt.[12]

That's not the way things should be. We ought to be able to look at a company's financial results and know that they haven't been massaged for weeks on end just so that the company can eke out another penny in earnings. We shouldn't have to pore over pages of 8-point print simply to figure out how options and pensions are propping up the bottom line.

Of course, in order to get more, we also need to start acting a lot more responsibly. Investing is serious business, and it requires a lot more thought than many of us—myself included—were giving it during the dot-com years. Once you begin to understand what you're looking for, devoting just a little more time to your investments each week can make a world of difference. For those investors who are just looking to have some fun, it makes a lot more sense to head to Las Vegas, where at least the odds are known and posted.

Simply hoping that prosecutors and regulators and Congress will be able to rout out or legislate against corporate fraud and overly aggressive accounting is a novel idea, but it's unlikely to work. "They'll never be able to legislate against dishonesty," says Robert Olstein. "They can come up with new ways to stop this, but people will come up with ways around it."

Then again, there are over 25,000 trees in Central Park.

A FEW FINAL WORDS

FOR MANY INVESTORS, this may very well be the first time that you are picking up a 10-K or 10-Q instead of the much shorter quarterly press release or glossy annual report. With its dense text and 8-point type, it will not just look different. It will feel different too. Even though some companies have begun to take serious steps to make their SEC filings a lot more readable for individual investors, these hefty documents can still be difficult for most people to get through.

The important thing is to start slow. Remember, Rome wasn't built in a day. Few of us, no matter how sophisticated an investor we are (or think we are), will be able to pick up these skills overnight. By reading this book, you have already invested some of your time, and perhaps, some of your money. But learning how to put these skills to work in the real world, with your own money at stake, will require a much bigger investment.

A few words of practical advice: Instead of sitting down with a stack of filings or plunking down in front of the computer and trying to read everything all at once, pick your spots. If you own stocks in several different companies, start with your largest holding, or the one that you secretly worry about most. Use some of the shortcuts discussed throughout this book to determine whether this particular company deserves a more thorough analysis. Downloading an SEC document onto your computer and searching for words such as "pension assumption" or "option exchange" or "related party" can often provide you with quick clues about the type of company you are dealing with and how aggressive they are when it comes to their accounting.

Even people who have been reading SEC filings for years—people like Warren Buffett who has said that he often reads one 10-K and several 10-Qs in a typical day—admit that many of these filings can be very complicated. Some, like Enron, are purposely designed that way. When that happens, the best thing to do is to simply walk away.

APPENDIX A

A Cheat Sheet for Reading Key SEC Filings

ANY INVESTOR WHO wants to pick their own stocks needs to feel comfortable reading, or at least skimming, a company's 10-Q, 10-K, and proxy statement. Companies file 10-Qs three times a year, usually about a month after the end of their first, second, and third quarters. Information for the fourth quarter is included in the 10-K, a much more detailed version of the annual report that typically comes out two to three months after the end of the fiscal year. Many companies either post these reports or provide links on their own web sites. They are also available on the SEC's Edgar database at *www.sec.com/edgar* and on several subscription-based web sites, including *www.10kwizard.com.* Companies file proxy statements annually and typically send a copy to investors in the mail, although they may be available sooner electronically. Once you become familiar with these documents, looking for a few key items should not take much time—figure 20–30 minutes for a 10-Q and a proxy and an hour for a 10-K—and could save you a lot of money by helping you avoid potential problems early on. Remember, there is no need to read every word or even understand everything that you are reading. What you are looking for are signs of aggressive accounting and any significant changes that were not in the filing last quarter or last year. What makes something significant? That's difficult to say. In a way, it's similar to how the Supreme Court defines obscenity: you'll know it when you see it. With that in mind, here are a few suggestions on what to look for in these documents:

Quarterly

☐ How does net income compare with pro forma income? What is the company excluding to arrive at the pro forma number and does it make sense?

☐ Are there other sizable differences between the numbers reported in the quarterly earnings release and the 10-Q? (Hint: Pay particular attention to operating income, especially if the company describes this as operating earnings.)

☐ Is the company expensing its stock options? If not, how does earnings per share change once the cost of options are included? (Hint: Pay particular attention to the difference between earnings per share as reported and diluted pro forma earnings per share.)

☐ What sorts of things and how much is the company keeping off balance sheet?

☐ Are there any significant changes in the company's segment breakdown? Is the company reporting fewer segments than before?

☐ Are there any new commitments and contingencies?

10-K (in addition to the above questions)

☐ What interest rate is the company using to calculate its pension income?

☐ Has the company made any changes in the way it recognizes revenue?

☐ How is the company accounting for its restructuring charges? Are there large amounts of money that have yet to be used for restructuring?

☐ Are the company's deferred income taxes growing? What is the company's effective income tax rate?

☐ How is the company handling its debt? Is the new debt at favorable interest rates?

☐ What sorts of related party transactions is the company including and how does this compare to the disclosure in the proxy on related party transactions?

☐ What is the company including in its other assets/liabilities and other income/loss? Are derivatives a substantial component of these numbers?

☐ How has stockholders equity changed over the past year?

Proxy

- ☐ How many times did the audit committee meet in the past year? Does the audit committee seem to have enough experience and independence to ask tough questions of company management?

- ☐ What types of related party transactions are being disclosed? Has there been a substantial increase in these transactions? Do they seem reasonable?

- ☐ How much stock do executive officers own? What about the directors?

- ☐ Do executive salaries correspond in any way to the company's financial performance over the past year?

- ☐ Do the retirement benefits for executives (including pension benefits) seem excessive given the company's performance?

- ☐ How much is the company paying its accounting firm for nonaudit services? How does this compare to previous years?

- ☐ What sorts of shareholder proposals are being included in the proxy? Do they raise concerns about the company's approach to corporate governance?

APPENDIX B

A Brief Walk through Qwest's Fine Print

AFTER WATCHING A nearly $4,000 investment in Qwest Communications dwindle to under $500, I decided to go back and look at the company's 10-K filings to see what warning signs I could have picked up on, if only I had taken the time to do this in the first place. This idea is not all that different from the way a coach studies videotape of a game after a big loss, or a group of doctors does a post-mortem after a patient dies unexpectedly. While hindsight is always perfect, it took me less than an hour to skim the 1999 and 2000 10-Ks. In that time, I was able to find enough red flags, that, had I read this material when I should have, would have prompted me to sell the stock and net a tidy profit well before the bottom fell out. Roughly speaking, I estimate that the hour I didn't spend on research cost me about $5,500, a rate that few people can claim an hour of their time is worth.

For those unfamiliar with Qwest, it was another in a long line of upstart telecommunications companies until it purchased US

West, one of the original Baby Bells, in June 2000 for $40 billion. Even though many of its former competitors have long since gone out of business, Qwest continues to hang on, despite serious questions over its accounting practices from the Securities and Exchange Commission (SEC), federal prosecutors, and members of Congress. The company, which, like Enron and WorldCom, used Arthur Andersen as its accountants, has restated its earnings four separate times, totaling $2.21 billion, and announced in April 2003 that additional restatements were possible pending another review by new auditors.

Although the details are specific to Qwest, this exercise shows you how an ordinary investor can cut through the fluff typically found in an annual report and get a better understanding of the stocks that they own by reading the footnotes in the 10-K. While I was able to find more than 10 red flags in both filings, most investors shouldn't need to find that many to avoid a stock or sell it before the problems get worse. Note that all the red flags are listed in the order they appear in the filings.

10 RED FLAGS FROM QWEST'S 1999 10-K

1. Uses percentage of completion to recognize revenues on long-term construction contracts. (Note 2, Summary of Significant Accounting Policies)

2. The rate of depreciation for its fiber optic network ranges from 10 to 25 years. (Note 2)

3. Agrees to purchase $140 million in services from Global Crossing Ltd. as part of the US West's decision to terminate its merger agreement. (Note 2)

4. Takes large in-process research and development charges when it acquired LCI Inc. and EUNet in 1998. (Note 3, Mergers and Acquisitions)

5. Creates a company with a subsidiary of its principal shareholder, Anschutz Co., and agrees to purchase another company from Anschutz. (Note 4, Investments)

6. Discloses a $90 million investment in Advanced Radio Telecom Corp., an Internet service provider, and notes that in connection with this, "a separate group of investors" also invested $161 million, without describing who that group is or how it relates to Qwest. (Note 4)

7. Agrees to purchase services over the next seven years from Rhythms NetConnections, a company that it has invested in. If it does not purchase those services, Qwest says it is still on the hook. (Note 4)

8. Pays only $300,000 in taxes in 1999, despite reporting $458.5 million in income. Qwest defers nearly $125 million in taxes. It lists its income tax rate as 21.4 percent, well below normal range of 30 percent to 40 percent. (Note 8, Income Taxes)

9. Hints at sizable off-balance sheet obligations, which it lists as operating lease agreements. (Note 9, Commitments and Contingencies)

10. Stock options account for nearly 10 percent of outstanding shares available and, if expensed, would reduce net income to 52 cents a diluted share compared with the 63 cents Qwest reported. (Note 11, Stockholder's Equity)

10 RED FLAGS FROM QWEST'S 2000 10-K

1. Reported results differ substantially from those released two months earlier in its press release. In January 2001, the company reported pro forma net income of $995 million, but in the 10-K, the company notes that it actually lost $81 million for the year. (Note 1, Consolidated Statements of Operation)

2. Takes a more aggressive approach in the way it recognizes revenue from its yellow pages, which leads to a $240 million one-time gain, and from sales of capacity to other telecommunications providers. (Note 2, Summary of Significant Accounting Policies)

3. Uses the first-in first-out (FIFO) method to account for its inventories, which is generally considered to be more aggressive than last-in first-out (LIFO). (Note 2)

4. Uses 40 years to depreciate $28 billion in goodwill. (Note 2)

5. Sets up a derivatives contract that uses Global Crossing stock as a peg even though Qwest sold its stake in Global Crossing. (Note 2)

6. Lists depreciation rates for $19.3 billion in "other network equipment" as 8 to 57 years, giving management wide discretion on depreciation. (Note 3, Property, Plant and Equipment)

7. Increases both the discount rate and expected rate of return on pension assets, which makes plan obligations look smaller and plan returns look higher. (Note 6, Employee Benefits)

8. Lists its effective tax rate as 164.3 percent, which is highly unusual. It also gives numbers for 1999 taxes paid and tax rate that differ substantially from those included in the company's 1999 10-K. (Note 7, Income Taxes)

9. Notes that its reported loss would have doubled if options expenses has been factored in. (Note 8, Stockholder's Equity)

10. Outlines a "round-trip" deal with IBM Corp., where IBM agrees to purchase $2.5 billion in telecommunications services from Qwest and Qwest agrees to purchase $2.5 billion in equipment from IBM. (Note 9, Commitments and Contingencies)

NOTES

Chapter 1

1. Arthur Levitt with Paula Dwyer, *Take on the Street: What Wall Street and Corporate America Don't Want You to Know* (New York: Pantheon Books, 2002), p. 155.
2. Ronald Fink, "The Fear of All Sums" and "Better Numbers?" *CFO: The Magazine for Senior Financial Executives,* August 2002, pp. 34–42.
3. "Stock Fund Managers Focus on Bonds, Accounting," *Bloomberg News,* March 19, 2002.
4. Tyco International, 8-K, December 30, 2002, p. 4.
5. Tyco International, 1998 annual report, p. 38.

Chapter 2

1. "Some Myths Continue on Wall Street," Dow Jones News Service, October 23, 2002.
2. "Skilling, Analyst Verbally Butt Heads," *Houston Chronicle,* April 18, 2001.

3. "AOL Time Warner Discloses SEC Probe," *Washington Post,* July 25, 2002, p. A1.

4. U.S. Government Accounting Office, "Financial Statement Restatements: Trends, Market Impacts, Regulatory Responses, and Remaining Challenges," October 4, 2002, p. 5.

5. *Ibid.,* p. 17.

6. "Bristol-Myers Lowers Revenue by \$2.5 Billion in Restatement," *The New York Times,* March 11, 2003, p. C1.

Chapter 3

1. "Damage Control: How Messier Kept Cash Crisis at Vivendi Hidden for Months," *The Wall Street Journal,* October 31, 2001, p. A1.

2. Robert J. Bloomfield, "The Incomplete Revelation Hypothesis and Financial Reporting," *Accounting Horizons,* Vol. 16, No. 3, September 2002, pp. 233–243.

3. "Footnote Trim Meets Mixed Response," *Austin-American Statesman,* October 22, 1995, p. G4.

4. *Ibid.*

5. Steven Milunovich, "TechStart Barometer," Merrill Lynch, April 26, 2002, pp. 5–6.

Chapter 4

1. "'Pro Forma' Financial Information: Tips for Investors," U.S. Securities and Exchange Commission, December 4, 2001.

2. Warren Buffett, annual letter to shareholders, Berkshire Hathaway 2002 annual report, pp. 3-4.

3. "P&G to Stop Reporting Dual Sets of Results," *The New York Times*, December 13, 2003, p. C4.

4. Arthur Levitt, "The Numbers Game," speech at New York University, September 28, 1998.

5. Cynthia A. Glassman, speech to Financial Executives International, 2002 annual conference, November 5, 2002.

6. "Ouch! Real Numbers," *Business Week*, March 24, 2003, p. 72.

7. "Motorola's Profit: 'Special' Again?" *The Wall Street Journal*, October 15, 2002, p. C1.

8. T. J. Rodgers, "When Accountants Attack Profits: The GAAP Accounting Exodus," position paper based on speech to Stanford Directors College, June 3, 2002.

9. "'Goodwill' Is Not an Option: Against Accounting Change," *The Wall Street Journal*, Manager's Journal, March 4, 2003.

10. Russell Lundholm, Jeff Doyle, and Mark Soliman, "The Predictive Value of Expenses Excluded from Pro Forma Earnings," University of Michigan Business School. Working Paper, April 2002.

11. "Earnings Purity and Stock Performance," Baseline Financial Services, April 2003, pp. 7–8.

12. "Pro Forma Earnings: A Critical Perspective," Bear Stearns & Co., September 2002, pp. 5-6.

Chapter 5

1. Kodak, 2001 10-K filing, footnote 18, p. 73. March 30, 2002.

2. Bear Stearns & Co., "Employee Stock Option Expense: Is the Time Right for Change?" July 2002.

3. Yahoo! 2001 Annual Report, footnote 8, pp. 58–59.

4. Arthur Levitt with Paula Dwyer, *Take on the Street: What Wall Street and Corporate America Don't Want You to Know* (New York: Pantheon Books, 2002), p. 11.

5. Warren Buffett, annual letter to shareholders, in Berkshire Hathaway 1998 annual report, p. 12.

6. Warren Buffett, annual letter to shareholders, in Berkshire Hathaway 2002 annual report, p. 20.

7. "Lawmakers Ask SEC to Evaluate Options Pricing Model," Dow Jones News Service, March 21, 2003.

8. "Senators Introduce Bill to Defer Stock-Option Expensing," Dow Jones News Service, April 29, 2003.

9. IBM Corp., 2003 proxy statement, pp. 31–32.

10. "Silicon Valley Fights Fiercely for Options," *San Francisco Chronicle*, November 10, 2002, p. G1.

11. Cisco, 10-Q, November 21, 2002, p. 8.

12. Citizens for Tax Justice, "Less than Zero: Enron's Income Tax Payments, 1996–2002," January 2002.

13. M. Sullivan, "Let the Good Times Roll: Options and Tax-free Profits," *Tax Notes*, May 29, 2000, pp. 1185–1204.

14. Bear Stearns, "Employee Stock Option Expense," p. 19.

15. FAS 148, "Accounting for Stock-Based Compensation—Transition and Disclosure," December 2002.

Chapter 6

1. HealthSouth, 2001 10-K, p. 64.

2. Enron Corp., 1999 annual report, p. 59.

3. FAS 57, "Related Party Disclosures," March 1982.

4. Enron Corp., proxy statement, March 30, 1999, p. 27.

5. WorldCom, proxy statement, June 1, 2000, p. 16.

6. "SEC Charges Adelphia & Rigas Family with Massive Financial Fraud," SEC press release, July 24, 2002.

7. "Fallen Founder of Adelphia Tries to Explain," *The New York Times*, April 7, 2003, p. C1.

8. "The TSC Streetside Chat: Adelphia Watcher Oren Cohen," TheStreet.com, April 6, 2002.

9. "Family Affairs: Rite Aid Does Business with Firms Linked to CEO Martin Grass," *The Wall Street Journal*, January 29, 1999, p. A1.

10. Rite Aid Corp., proxy statement, October 24, 2000, p. 31.

11. Tyco International, proxy statement, February 7, 2003, pp. 48–49.

12. HealthSouth, proxy statement, April 12, 2002, p. 13.

13. "My Big Fat Corporate Loan," The Corporate Library, December 2002.

14. Hewlett-Packard, 2002 10-K, p. 445.

15. "H-P Severance Curbs Get Holder Support," *The Wall Street Journal*, April 3, 2003, p. B5.

Chapter 7

1. "FASB Members Get Input on Pension Accounting Rules," Dow Jones News Service, February 14, 2003.

2. "GM Outlines Objectives for 2003," GM press release, January 9, 2003.

3. "Beware the Pension Monster," *Fortune*, December 9, 2002, p. 99.

4. "The Quarterly Report: Second Quarter 2003," Credit Suisse First Boston, April 14, 2003, pp. 7–8.

5. "As Steel Industry Consolidates, Workers' Benefits Begin to Shift," *The Wall Street Journal*, January 13, 2003, p. A3.

6. "Beware the Pension Monster," *Fortune*, December 9, 2002, p. 99.

Chapter 8

1. Yahoo!, 2001 annual report, p. 2.

2. *Ibid.*, p. 44.

3. U.S. Bankruptcy Court, Southern District of New York. *In re:* Enron Corp. et al., "Second Interim Report of Neal Batson, Court Appointed Examiner," January 21, 2003, p. 47.

4. "Tales of the Tape: Expect Some Off-Balance Surprises," Dow Jones News Service, February 4, 2003.

5. Citigroup, 2002 10-K, p. 99.

6. GE Capital Corporate Aircraft group web site: *www.cefcorp.com/aircraft/offbalance.htm.*

7. Lucent Technologies, 1999 10-K, p. 99.

8. Arthur Levitt with Paula Dwyer, *Take on the Street: What Wall Street and Corporate America Don't Want You to Know* (New York: Pantheon Books, 2002), p. 149.

9. Lucent Technologies, 1999 10-K, p. 117.

Chapter 9

1. "Gap Grows Between Book and Tax Income," *The Wall Street Journal*, July 16, 2002, p. D4.

2. "Enron Cut Tax Bill by $2 Billion in Working Around IRS Rules," *The Wall Street Journal*, February 14, 2003, p. A2.

3. Enron Corp., 1999 annual report, p. 50.

4. General Electric, 2002 10-K, Notes to Consolidated Financial Statements, p. F-45.

5. Indrani De Basak and Michelle R. Clayman, "Tax Rates and Stock Returns: An Empirical Analysis of the Information Content of Corporate Tax Rates," New Amsterdam Partners LLC., February 2003, p. 5.

6. Citigroup, 2002 10-K, Glossary of Terms, p. 60.

7. Warren Buffett, annual letter to shareholders, in Berkshire Hathaway 2002 annual report, pp. 13–15.

8. *Ibid.*

9. "Divided on Derivatives; Greenspan, Buffett at Odds on Risks of the Financial Instruments," *Washington Post*, March 6, 2003, p. E1.

10. IBM, 2002 10-K, Consolidated Statement of Earnings, p. 64.

11. General Electric, 2002 10-K, Statement of Financial Position, p. F33.

12. IBM, 2002 10-K, Management's Discussion and Analysis, p. 52.

13. IBM, 2002 10-K, Notes to Consolidated Statements, Note S, Subsection E, p. 91.

14. IBM, 2000 10-K, Management's Discussion and Analysis, p. 57.

15. "Altria Verdict Unnerves Market with Possible Bankruptcy Filing," *The Wall Street Journal*, April 1, 2003.

16. Boeing, 2002 10-K, Notes to Consolidated Financial Statements, pp. 81–82.

17. Sun Microsystems, 2003 fiscal first quarter 10-Q, p. 13.

18. Caterpillar Corp., 2002 10-K, Notes to Consolidated Financial Statements, p. A-24.

Chapter 10

1. Remarks on signing the Sarbanes-Oxley Act of 2002. Cited in "Weekly Compilation of Presidential Documents," August 5, 2002.

2. "Scrushy Tape Played in Court During Hearing," Reuters, April 10, 2003.

3. "Do We Really Want to Trash All of That?" *The Wall Street Journal*, April 12, 2003. Partial transcript of tape-recorded conversation between Richard Scrushy and William Owens.

4. "Better Numbers," *CFO: The Magazine for Senior Financial Executives*, August 2002, p. 38.

5. PricewaterhouseCoopers Management Barometer, March 24, 2003.

6. "HealthSouth Ex-Executive Is Charged," *The New York Times*, April 9, 2003, p. C1.

7. HealthSouth, 2002 proxy, p. 7.

8. *Ibid.*, p. 5.

9. *Ibid.*, p. 21.

10. Securities and Exchange Commission, Division of Corporation Finance, "Summary by the Division of Corporation Finance of Significant Issues Addressed in the Review of the Periodic Reports of the Fortune 500 Companies," February 27, 2003.

11. Paul S. Atkins, speech before the Council of Institutional Investors, March 27, 2003.

12. Arthur Levitt with Paula Dwyer, *Take on the Street: What Wall Street and Corporate America Don't Want You to Know* (New York: Pantheon Books, 2002), p. 237.

INDEX

Printed and bound by CPI Group (UK) Ltd, Croydon, CR0 4YY

16/04/2025

14658522-0001